I0152369

REFERENCE POINT

BY MICHAEL HURD

Copyright © 2017

Reference Point (c) 2017, Michael Hurd
ISBN: 978-0-9950518-2-9
ISBN EBook: 978-0-9950518-3-6

All rights reserved. No part of this book may be reproduced, stored in a retrieval system, or transmitted, in any form or by any means, electronic, mechanical, photocopying, recording, or otherwise, without prior written permission of the copyright owner.

ISBN 978-0-9950518-2-9

90000

9 780995 051829

i hold a secret within me,
one about which you must never ask.
were you not the one who first revealed it?

Table of Contents: Page

Prologue

Let's get reacquainted. We are *The Gathering*, and we have been communicating with you through this reading process. We've introduced you to various ideas and characters in order to help you get *Home*. Since our last set of communications, you have been adjusting to everything you have read, and you are also reading other books.

You are on the right track.

We will not be repeating everything from the first book, because it has already been said, and you can refer to it anytime you like. Having read the first message, the title of this book will not surprise you. These new *Articles* will draw you closer to *The Reference Point* and *Home*. Do you feel ready to continue? Your imagination has been very busy all this while, wondering what the experience of *The Reference Point* might be like. You have even done some practicing with respect to imagining carrying on *Home,* without the need for our help. You should continue to do this. As you draw closer to it, it is only natural that you would begin to adopt some of its attitudes and views. *The Reference Point* is guiding you to itself. It is *more* than simply a time and a place.

You should also know that Bax has returned to us.

Article Four:

The
Revealing

1

Prepare yourself for the *Unexpected*. You have your own, personal ways for doing this, and we respect them. Now, simply focus your attention with us, as we take you deeper into mystery...

This book is like a doorway, one of the ones in your memory that you eventually wanted to open.

Now, the time is right.

Take a moment to familiarize yourself with the way the book feels in your hands. How does it appear to you? Do you sense that this book is somehow different from the last? Can you describe how? What are your hopes, your predictions, for this reading?

We know, we are already asking a lot of questions. But, is that not what friends do, when time has passed between visits? We will not ask you how you have been, because we already know. At the same time, we will not tell you how *we* are doing because it is all the same.
As you will come to understand, *The Revealing* is an important part of the journey *Home*. We could have placed this article towards the end of the book, but because of its importance with respect to meeting the *Reference Point*, we could not allow it to wait much longer. Time seems to be speeding-up for you and the others.

The Revealing is probably best described as a process of transformation. It's a big change in the way that things will appear in *Reality*. Some might say it's a complete overhaul of *Reality*, itself! Fortunately, that's not the case. As you already know, just because something starts to look and act differently, doesn't mean that they're actually different from what they were. They're all just changes in wardrobe, setting, and so on. It's me Bax, by the way. Your ability to focus-in on our communication has brought me onto the page more quickly than anticipated. Your ability to focus has improved!

As the title indicates, *The Revealing* will show you things. It will do this many times, by taking something else away. This is different from just substituting one thing for another. You won't be trading any images during *The Revealing*; you'll be going inside, you'll be looking deeper. It will do this, so that you can see what's underneath. Being underneath, it was previously hidden from you. At times, you might have felt that it was lost to you, but nothing is ever really lost.

Why was it hidden? By whom? *Reality* likes to show you the things you want to see, the things that relate to your program. Now that you've decided you want to see something else, *Reality* will try to accommodate you. This can lead to a mixture of things happening in your lifetime, the things you originally wanted to see, versus those you *now* wish to see. As you can imagine, this can lead to chaos and confusion. You can reduce the confusion by focusing on one, *or* the other. You can decide to stick with your original program for this lifetime, or you can focus on returning *Home*.

If you try to have both, you'll soon find that very little gets accomplished in this lifetime. This will lead to personal frustration. It's a feeling that many of us face. Being who we really are, we naturally want to choose both, instead of 'either/or.' That's because we're familiar with having it all. Before entering *Reality*, we never had to choose between one thing, or another. We're able to sense this, and it leads to a feeling of dissatisfaction with *Reality*, even though *Reality* tries its best to compensate.

Mixed messages lead to mixed results.

Reality doesn't really mind which you choose, as long as you're happy. But, because it is limited in its ability to adjust to your experience here, it's having trouble keeping up with everyone's mixed messages and changing requests. This is a good thing for you and the others! You're overloading the system so much, the picture is beginning to destabilize. This weakening effect is what's now showing you new, unexpected and hidden things. It's leading you to the truth. It's leading you all *Home*.

The 'mixed messages' phase will only last for a while. As your focus and the desire to return *Home* improve, things will appear to re-stabilize. When they do, everything will seem different. *Reality* will have adjusted to your new plan, the one that brings you *Home*. *Reality* won't be aware of this, it will simply think that it has granted your wishes.

I'd like to say that a change is coming, but we both know that change is really a constant in your world. The only thing about change that isn't constant, is how each of us experiences it, or takes part in it. We each play different roles in the process, and at different times. For some, the effects of change seem more difficult than others. That's one reason we're all here.

We're here, for one another.

The changes will be experienced in ways that are both personal and shared. Understanding this, we're less likely to question the reactions and responses of the others, and more open to supporting and assisting them. You are one of the many for whom the changes will begin to appear first. *The Revealing* will begin gently, and you'll recognize its appearance in due time. Of course, there will be some who don't notice its beginnings. For them *The Revealing* may seem startling. Someone will attend to them when this happens. It might be you.

2

What is it you'll be seeing, in the times ahead?

You won't *see* anything.

In this world, we can only perceive, or watch. Seeing is more than these. It's a big part of the awareness of being *Home*. This is because seeing involves *The Truth*. Since *The Truth* never changes, if you were to actually *see*, that which you were seeing would always be the same. In this world, you perceive that everything changes.

Perceiving is the same as collecting. In *Reality*, we collect. We use everything we collect, in order to build pictures, sound and other sensations that inform our experience of this world. We can also compare all that we collect, with what we've previously collected, to find similarities and differences. Making further connections with all of these collections, allows us to build a steady stream of moments to form a lifetime.

Our perceptions are limited for a purpose. They're *narrowed*, so that we're better able to focus on those particular things that relate to our programs. Without these limits your human body would go into overload, and malfunction. The conditions of quick-pacing and overstimulation in your time, give you a hint of what i've just said. Feeling overstimulated lately? This is connected with the 'mixed messages' topic i mentioned earlier.

We're trying to get the most out of this lifetime.

You've probably already noticed that when I speak of 'we' and 'our', it's a little different from the previous book. In *this* book, these terms more often point to you and me, rather than *The Gathering*. My human experiences have brought us into relationship.

In *Reality*, we don't really need to see, because seeing would provide us with much that isn't useful for this experience. The senses we *do* possess, actually offer us more than we realize. Our collections are filled with items that didn't originally 'fit' with what we understood, or recognized. These items are in storage and can be brought up to the *attention space*. This is done automatically, once they eventually match with our understanding. Some of these items have been in storage a very long time. When they do arrive, we feel a sense of 'a-ha!' in the moment of their arrival. We might even ask ourselves:

Why didn't i realize this before?

Now, you know why. *Now* you know that you have everything you need for the journey *Home* either in storage, or in your present awareness. Time and experience will help you get there.

After the 'a-ha!' realization, you can't go back to looking at the world in quite the same manner. Things have changed in an important way. Things have changed for the better. It won't always seem that way, especially if the realization connects you with feelings of regret, or sadness about the way they happened before that moment. The choices you made were based on what you believed in those previous moments. Now, you can do things differently. i know about these feelings, and i know what it's like to wish that i could have done things differently. If only i had known.

i hope this puts your mind at ease.

Through this continuing process, you'll begin to look at the world in new ways. And, because your way of viewing the world will change, the world *itself* will appear to change. You are the agents of change, in your world. i understand this sounds like added responsibility, but the process will be gradual. It will only require small steps. If you're going to be successful, the steps must be continuous. We can't stop and we can't ever give-up.

What happens if you start to notice the world is changing in ways you don't like, or can't stand to witness? Know that the effect will be a temporary one and that another will soon replace it. In addition, what you're witnessing can be taken from you, to reveal what's underneath, or hidden within it. You might be asked to take action in the midst of what you're experiencing, in order to correct the situation. Correction is needed, if you prefer that revealing happens rather than replacing, or substituting. It's a lot to consider.

You know what you want.

Something else happens while all of this is going on. You begin to look at *yourself* in new ways, too! The understanding of who and what you believe yourself to be won't stay the same. The ideas around believing in yourself as a 'person,' the body you inhabit and the lifetime you experience, start to shift. They grow in a way that allows you to believe that you're something more than what you've been told. It's not 'more' in the way that overemphasizes your personal importance, but one that enriches your understanding of who and what you truly are, beyond the experience of *Reality*. Reaching this understanding improves your interactions with others and increases the level of enjoyment within *Reality*, which improves *Reality* itself! Is this beginning to make good sense?

There are many things collected by your senses which seem so unusual, so foreign to you, that they require a fair amount of progress on the journey *Home* before you can appreciate them. They don't quite fit with your understanding right now, but you're getting closer to them. Keep going; they're important.

3

Your human senses can mislead you. They aren't doing it on purpose, it's just the way they are. Because of this, you'll need to lead yourself. When i say this, i mean that you should pay attention to what you're collecting. Accept what's helpful for you and discard anything that's potentially harmful. Helpful items are anything that fits with your program, or with your returning *Home*. If you should accidentally throw away something that's helpful, don't worry. It will come back to you.

As you start 'scratching the surface' of *Reality*, you'll begin to really appreciate how things are. Many things will begin to feel less important than originally believed. You might even begin to recognize that much in which you first believed, has now turned towards its opposite. This includes some of your personal relationships, too. Thankfully, many new things and relationships will reveal themselves as having *more* significance for you.

i wouldn't want you to feel that your lifetime was entirely pointless.

The things and people who reveal themselves with greater meaning and significance will more than compensate you for any apparent loss of those others. Your lifetime will be much more enjoyable.

Farther along, some of you might begin to experience a sense that *everything* has changed around your perception. This happens to some people. It's as if they've started their lifetime all over again. The way they act and speak makes them seem like a very different person. When this happens, you may be tempted to try and reverse the changes in them. You might worry that you're losing someone close to you. You haven't lost them. They're still with you, and they still remember you. Sometimes, the best we can do, is support them in these new choices. If the choices are helpful, they will benefit everyone. If they prove harmful, they won't last. All harmful things and relationships are never meant to last, in *Reality*. They go against the most important reason for being here, to enjoy yourself. *Reality* doesn't allow them to exist beyond a certain level.

This was something i experienced during one of my lifetimes. When i reached a certain age, i remembered myself as being one among *The Gathering*. i remembered that i was Bax, who chose to enter *Reality* in order to help with the journey *Home*. It was quite a surprise when it happened, and it disrupted many of the relationships i had formed. People weren't happy about my new way of living. They didn't agree with my ideas and they certainly didn't want me sharing them with others. That was a quick lifetime.

i returned later, with better results.

Speaking in the outward sense of the things you perceive as being outside of your body, you may experience moments where you find yourself 'looking twice', to be sure of what's happening in front of you. How might you feel about visions from the past, or the future? Would you be interested in meeting with beings from another time, or place? (There are other worlds.) Would you be upset about your dreaming world mixing together with your waking world? Many things are possible in *The Revealing*. These are only three of them. If they were to happen to you, you would be ready. You would recognize them for what they are, symptoms of your growing ability to look deeper into *Reality*. Your degree of perception is gently opening, and with it, the size of your *attention space*. As this happens, more and more information will make itself available to you. Choose to keep and use what's helpful. You shouldn't be filling this extra space with more distractions. It's growing so that you can focus on bigger challenges, without becoming overwhelmed.

For some time now, the first hints of these *Revealing* perception experiences have been showing up as the 'déjà vu.' These are very common among you, but you tend to 'shrug' them off and continue on with whatever you happen to be doing. They're amusing at the time, but you're not quite sure what they are. Pay more attention to them when they arrive. Try to gently hold on to them, while they're happening. You can do this by noticing everything about them, everything your perception is telling you. Then, gently let the experience go. Why am i telling you this? First of all, so the experiences will last longer and second, so you can learn about time.

You're developing a central point of balance within yourself, so that unusual events don't cause you to stumble. You're becoming more stable, which decreases the amount of distraction and confusion in your lifetime. As you continue to participate in the action, your emotions will begin to resist the highs and lows of all the drama, bringing a lasting peacefulness and calm to your days.

If you ever want to know how well you're doing on the journey *Home*, just take a look around you. What is your perception telling you?

It speaks to your belief, about who you are.

4

You're not alone in *Reality*. There are many others with you, enjoying what they can of their programs. All of them are acting. Some of them realize they are acting, many do not. *The Revealing* will improve upon this.

With your perception of *Reality* deepening, and following with your ability to face new and unusual challenges, the others will begin to undergo a transformation. At first, the differences will be noticed 'inside' of them. People will start to feel differently about the world; their opinions will start to change. Then, many will start to notice changes happening on the 'outside.' This will be the natural order of events in *The Revealing.*

First within - then without.

You'll often want to speak to someone right away, about these perceptual changes. It's an exciting time. But, i'm going to ask you to be patient for a while. You might be one of the first to notice the changes, and telling someone might alarm them enough that they would question you about proof. There won't be any proof to offer, at first. Knowing that the body doesn't wish to lie, you'll be able to notice signs of distress in others, especially in their facial expressions. This will be your cue. i asked for patience about telling people about your own perceptions, but that doesn't mean you can't ask them questions about theirs. If someone looks distressed and the reasons aren't apparent, introduce yourself. Ask them what they're feeling, right now. If they answer you, you can then begin to ask them additional questions about the experience they're having. If they aren't ready to answer your questions, simply let them know that you understand how challenging it can be to describe certain experiences, and that you're available, should they need to reach you.

Chances are, they don't know about *The Revealing* process. They may not know that they've started opening to a larger picture of *Reality*. The others will benefit from our listening. Later, they will begin asking questions. They'll want to fill those gaps in their understanding. These experiences don't always agree with what we would consider as 'normal'. This will be another cue for you. You can begin speaking, little-by-little, about what you believe. Because of the lack of proof, we won't be able to say that we *know* what's happening. We can only say that we believe a particular thing is occurring, or has materialized.

We should only express possibilities and opinions. This opens a space for discussion, and values equality between persons. We are equals in this process. None of us can truthfully say that they have an advantage, that would enable them to take control over our experience of *The Revealing*. As persons, it's much bigger than any one of us.

In this world, we sometimes want to feel like experts. The world is very competitive in its social design. Information appears to have value, and possessing it seems connected with power. *Reality* appears to reward those who possess these elements within the structure of their program. Every program has its benefits and challenges, no matter how things might appear. When a person lives according to their program, the benefits and challenges are designed to cancel each other out. This is a service feature within *Reality* that helps to maintain a balance within and between human experiences. When we achieve this balance, we have a better chance of returning *Home* satisfactorily. Customer satisfaction is achieved within *Reality*, in many different ways. The ways i've mentioned previously, focused on keeping you here. But, there are others that will encourage you to return to *Reality*, simply because the previous visits were so enjoyable.

When you find yourself with distressed others, it's not an accident. A scene will unfold before you. You will have your lines, you'll be in character and the previously mentioned cues will start to arrive. If you are the one showing distress, another will attend to your needs. Even if there is a language barrier between you, or the other arrives from origins unknown, you will be present for each other and feel that everything's happening as it should. In those moments, we start to forget about any ideas of 'friend' or 'enemy,' understanding the others now, as familiar.

5

You will begin to hear many sounds. Within *Reality*, the process of change needs to involve sound. The reason sound was included, was so that you could connect the sounds with any images you faced. The two go very well together, in the production process.

Your hearing senses, just like your visual ones, are limited. They're limited for the exact same reasons. The sounds you will eventually begin to notice, won't always be connected with the images you're facing. You'll start to search for the source of these noises, but you won't find them. You'll want to tell others about these sounds, but it's probably best to wait. The sounds relate to changes that are happening 'behind the scenes' of *Reality*. Try as they might, the 'stage hands' of *Reality* can't always move things quietly, during a performance. Occasionally, the actors and the audience will notice what's being done. i understand this can be distracting.

This also describes what will be happening during the *The Revealing*. You'll be one of the ones in the audience, or on stage, who can hear the adjustments being made to *Reality*. Usually, the changes happen more gradually, when it's easier for *Reality* to do so. Because the changes will be happening more frequently and more drastically, there's going to be some noise and disturbance. The ones who are caught-up in the drama won't notice, so much. But, because *your* view of the situation has grown, you'll register these changes.

Knowing the source and purpose of these sounds should put you at ease. They don't represent any real danger to anyone. Because the sounds aren't connected with any known visual stimulus, they will seem unfamiliar. It's those unfamiliar ones that tend to startle us, at first.

It won't be possible to record these sounds using mechanical devices. Those simple devices can only hear. *You* have the ability to listen. When you're not concerned with all the distractions of *Reality*, your perception can begin to offer something beyond the limits of your physical senses. Your body's design was originally guided by the parameters of your program. You're not your body, so you aren't guided by the same parameters. You're capable of greater perception, while you're here, but only in stages. The reason for the need to offer enhancements in stages has to do with altering the design of your human body. Imagine the process as one of 'tailoring' the body to suit your needs. *Reality* will perform any needed improvements, based on your choices and your needing to perceive certain things, at certain times. During the upgrades, you'll notice that your body feels tired. Let it rest.

Here's a small exercise that will help you in the development of your listening abilities.

Focus on the quiet spaces, between the noises, you're hearing.

If you'd also like an exercise for your visual abilities, i would suggest you begin by closing your eyelids. Using your imagination and your pressure sense, picture the position of your body in this moment. Draw an imaginary line around the contours of this image. Now connect that image with what you remember about your current surroundings. Gradually open your eyelids. Well done.

i understand any potential feelings of confusion you might be feeling, around the notion of exercising your visual perception with your eyelids closed. The exercise doesn't seem logical. To help ease these feelings, i'll just say that your eyes are only one of the tools involved with visual processing.

6

The Revealing can also be imagined as one's emerging out of a very, deep sleep. This is something you understand. A deep sleep can be so enjoyable, so restful, we often have to struggle to fully awaken ourselves. The temptation to return to that feeling of 'elsewhere' can be very strong. Experiences within *The Dreaming* also permit us abilities not commonly possessed in the waking world. This is the very thing that will be happening to us, when *The Revealing* arrives. We'll be caught up in that feeling of *elsewhere*, wanting to enjoy a few minutes more.

Reality is your *elsewhere*.

Preparing for *The Revealing* can sometimes lead to feelings of isolation, or loneliness. That's mainly due to its personal approach. Because the experience will be so specific, at times you might feel as if you're the only one involved. One of the reasons you came to visit *Reality* was so that you could feel what it's like to have a private self. You wanted to be a person with their own thoughts and feelings, who occasionally shared them with others. The amount you shared these thoughts and feelings ended up being directly connected with the amount of enjoyment you experienced here. More sharing meant more fun. But, this ultimately takes away from your sense of being a private person. *Now* you try to find a good balance between the two, in order to satisfy the goals of your program. Deep down, you know that sharing with others is the most natural thing you can do. It reminds you of *Home*. Occasional feelings of loneliness will not last, and they will be supported with the satisfaction and hope of understanding their purpose for a brighter future.

These feelings are also a side effect of something else that's happening. Whether you believe it or not, you are experiencing a form of grief. With each passing day, you feel like you might be losing a little something, or a little part of someone. They aren't actually being lost, they're simply in the process of changing. They aren't what they were. The changes appear two-sided, which leads to mixed emotions. You often feel glad of the new improvements, but sad of the separation from what you used to have, or used to be. The greater part of these feelings of grief relate to your person. You're growing at an incredible rate! You are grieving the loss of these old ideas about your person, while at the same time enjoying the benefits of a wider view.

By the same token, the others will be feeling the same loneliness and strangeness about you. They might even try to force you to stop all of this 'insane' growing. They'll try using guilt and bribery, and any number of tricks, to get you to stay the way you are. It won't work, at least not for long. We can't stop *The Revealing*. Accepting this, you'll need to get ready for it. It's too late to turn back. Frankly, i'm really looking forward to all the changes! If they get you closer to being back with us, i won't stand in their way. You've been gone so long.

7

A part of you might be starting to feel suspicious about *The Gathering* and its motives, regarding the journey *Home*. This part of you would protest that you hardly know us, especially in comparison to your friends and family. Who's to say that our encouragement of these changes isn't part of some dangerous plan for the human race?

You're the one to say.

As an intelligent collector, you're able to personally verify any and all of what i'm saying to you. Equally, you're able to disregard what you wish.

i'm not forcing you to believe in everything i tell you, nor to follow through with my recommendations for your future. The language i use however, might seem to imply this. It's an unfortunate limitation in how we're communicating right now. If you should ever sense that i'm pressuring you in any way, always remember that my duty is to inform. The perceived connections between information and power have already been mentioned, and might account for any sense of feeling 'coerced.'

It's easy to be fooled by many events, perceptions and people in *Reality*. You've learned this lesson well. But, it has made you more cautious and less trusting in some ways. While you were learning this lesson, you were also discovering that by paying attention, you could separate the important from the trivial, 'pretend' from the truth. You no longer needed to follow anyone else's beliefs and opinions about the world. You didn't have to borrow perspectives because you had your own, and you could rely on yourself. Achieving this, others can now rely on *you*. I call this moving toward sanity.

You'll know whom to trust.

The others will also know whom to trust. They'll invest their trust in *you*. Have you noticed that complete strangers are starting to confide in you? This is the kind of responsibility you'll want, as you prepare for *The Revealing*. Embrace it. It might just be the most satisfying part of your role. Trustworthy people are so valuable, especially during times of crisis.

People will slowly gravitate toward you. If the approach has not been gentle, feel free to openly question their motives. The more gentler approaches tend to reveal the presence of a sympathetic character. i'm using 'sympathetic' in the sense of their being similar to, or understanding of your nature. They may not even realize *why* they feel drawn to you. If you feel similarly drawn to them, read it as important. It may represent a connection with completing this lifetime's program, or the resolving of previous lifetime's obligations. The purposes will reveal themselves, eventually. These kinds of attractions (romantic, or otherwise) can help with any previously mentioned feelings of loneliness that might happen.

You will need some time alone. It's a form of rest. i learned to appreciate it, while human. Try not to confuse 'alone' with 'lonely.' They're quite different. As well, the 'lonely' are not 'bored.' Many people complain about loneliness, when they're really just bored and without company. These people usually crave entertainment, not the real solution to loneliness. Consider this, when are you least lonely? We'll look at two possibilities, for the purposes of this chapter. The first, happens when you are with other people who 'mirror' what you might be experiencing and feeling. The second is similar to the first.

You're least lonely, when you're most your Self.

Seems obvious, doesn't it? Sympathetic characters and the recognition that you're approaching the truth of who you are, will have many benefits on your wellbeing. Wait, this could lead to happiness, couldn't it? And, if you were happy, some of the others might not want to be around you anymore. This is because of their focus upon being miserable. If this should happen, you won't worry about it. You'll understand what's really happening. Your focus isn't their focus.

Your focus is telling you that:

misery doesn't actually love company, it just hates to be alone.

John Ray's[1] observations were accurate, based on what our human perception would suggest. But, everything's beginning to change for you. Your renewed focus is offering you something more.

Any reluctance to associate with unsympathetic others might make us seem cold and uncaring to them. More accurately, it isn't them we're rejecting. We're simply being drawn away from their preoccupations with matters unrelated to our new focus. They've likely gotten caught-up in *Reality's* drama. When they believe themselves to be justified in their unhappiness, it's doubtful that they are still following their programs. They might have gotten sidetracked, or distracted along the way. Your example will

---

[1] John Ray (1627-1705) English Naturalist, "misery loves company"

shed a bit of light on other options. Everything you do, influences others.

Over time, and even with your appearing to distance yourself from other people, *The Revealing* will bring us all closer together. That is one of its purposes. Any learned caution or lack of trust, has helped you to separate fact from fiction. The differences will soon be clear. This is when complete trust will finally return to you. It's the kind of trust you had when you were very young. Mistrust comes from doubt. When you remove the doubt from your perspective, trust returns.

We hope to find honesty in others. If we feel they're honest, we regain a general sense of trust in the world. The tendency to search for things outside of us, makes finding them more difficult. The next statement might seem strange.

It's difficult to find, what we don't already have.

Because the outside world can be a reflection of the inside world of our desires, imaginings and feelings, we need to first find the honesty within ourselves, before we'll truly find it in anyone else. *Reality* occasionally looks at your inner world, to help it design your outer experience for you. If we lie to ourselves, *Reality* will think (strangely) that *that's* the type of 'outer' world you're wanting to enjoy. Are you beginning to understand how powerful you are?

8

You're doing your best to be honest with yourself and it's helping to improve your situation. Honesty will happen in stages for many of you. As we open up to one belief about ourselves it leads us to other beliefs. With a keen eye to recognizing the truth, you'll realize which beliefs are correct. i don't want you to have any false beliefs about yourself.

With honesty, comes a certain feeling of seriousness around your personality. This is in part due to a growing feeling of importance about the things we say and do. You realize they have a big effect on the world, so you are taking more care. Things won't seem as funny, or carefree anymore. You will act seriously. This doesn't mean the same thing as acting serious. To act seriously is to take a little more responsibility for your part in the drama of *Reality*. You'll start to get all your lines right and you'll know to have certain props in place, to enhance the setting for what's about to happen. *The Revealing* will be something like a climax, or 'Grand finale' in *Reality*. Acting seriously won't feel like an extra burden for you. You'll easily adjust to the newness of it, and future events will seem to unfold according to a well-organized plan.

Each of you likes to follow a daily schedule of some sort. When things go according to plan, your day flows smoothly. Your daily routine will soon begin to follow a more natural plan, one that makes you happier. When we notice that our choices for the plan start to lead to problems, we gradually start to reduce the amount of control we extend toward organizing that plan.

Our old ways don't seem to be working.

This usually happens when we try to do too much. In doing this, we aren't leaving room for *The Unexpected*. It needs to be part of our day, too. Try as we might, we can't quite predict everything that will happen in a day. You're learning this quickly, and leaving more and more space to adapt to the unpredictable events of your lifetime. These events will begin to increase in number, but their effect will only be minor. You'll be able to manage them well.

Remembering this will help you to avoid feelings of frustration. If your frustration increases, so will your anger. Anger has a way of taking control over your person. Your body feels the anger building, and since it doesn't want to hold on to it, looks for a way to act on it. Physical activity helps the body get rid of the things it doesn't want, or can't safely hold. When this happens, you will feel as if you've been gently 'pushed aside' by the body, so that it can accomplish this. You won't feel that you're totally in control of the body during those moments. The results of these types of impulsive actions often lead to regret. This is one reason i want you to consider a more balanced pattern of activities for your day.

Not everyone will plan to organize their time in a balanced way, and you might get caught up in an event that results from an expression of their anger. The other person will appear to believe that their anger is directly related to you. They will blame you for their anger, saying that it's your fault. You'll perceive this to be false. Understanding what's happening, you'll feel fairly calm because you haven't been tricked into believing that their drama is real. This offers you better control within the situation, control over what you do. Your words and actions will be based on a choice of responses, rather than any uncontrolled reactions. Based on what someone chooses to do or say in these moments, the reactions of another can be guided in ways that are helpful.

Results aren't always guaranteed; however, because the other person might not accept the advice. Any offered assistance is valuable, even if the direct results aren't what you'd hoped. You're making a change in *Reality* that is unexpected, and these tend to have lasting effects. They release *indirect* results. The indirect ones produce a gradual effect that lasts longer for the intended audience. Yes, you'll be influencing more than one person. They're subtle suggestions, and because of this, they can enter into another's perception more easily. They bypass the other person's perceptual defenses through momentary distraction. Instead of immediately rejecting your assistance, as something expected and predictable, the other person considers it for a second. This second's hesitation is all you need, to get your point across. Once your unexpected ideas are planted within another person, they get to work.

True, the other person could reject your ideas later, but by the time they remember what you did or said, it'll be too late for their rejection to make any difference. The other person has already become someone new. Loud, disruptive messages can be easily rejected by people.

Careful, quiet messages are most effective.

During periods of confusion and chaos, when old concepts of the world are dying and new ones are beginning, you might notice that you feel a sense of relief. All of your efforts are starting to make a difference. Humans prefer instant results. They tend to offer us a reward, right away. They encourage us. But, as *The Gathering* mentioned in the first book, 'we want these improvements to last.' Instant results don't always last; they tend to have a rebound effect, that puts things right back to the way they were. Then we need to start the work all over again, which is very discouraging.

The sense of relief that comes to you, when you see the world changing for the better, gives you the courage to continue in the direction you've chosen. Your new beliefs and attitudes will bring a freshness to your experience. The information being gathered through perception won't have changed all that much, but the way you interpret this information will have grown. These new interpretations are producing that 'freshness' you're feeling.

Interpretation is a critical part of perception. Interpretation relies on your beliefs about the information you're collecting. For example, if we believe something is a weapon, as opposed to a tool, this will affect our interpretation and expectation of what's about to happen. Similarly, if we connect the item with the person holding it, we will decide if they are using it to build, or destroy. Our responses will quickly emerge out of these interpretations.

Perception is the information collected, as interpreted through our beliefs.

Since your beliefs act like a 'lens' for your interpretation process, it was decided that i should reach out to all of you on *that* level of perception. Everyone's very good at collecting and interpreting data, but the world's belief systems are currently too diverse to allow for a shared vision of the future. Your various beliefs are producing too many different outcomes, while at the same time, you're hoping that others will see things *your* way, in order to bring the world together. i'm going to help with this. i won't need *everyone* to agree with me in order to change perception, either. It doesn't have to be unanimous. The way i'm going to help with this is by adjusting *how* you believe, not what. If we focus on the goal, the ways for achieving it can be as diverse as we want.

9

Humans seem to be very focused upon *what* to believe. This hasn't led to any significant progress in getting you all *Home*. As a result, *The Revealing* was established. All of you have contributed to the conditions in *Reality* that will bring *The Revealing* into production. We can't point to any one group of people for its arrival. If we really consider it, everyone wants to return *Home*. You aren't entirely happy in *Reality*. The struggle and the drama have lost their appeal.

The Revealing will be unavoidable. That's not to say however, that it will be difficult. Each of you will experience it in a certain way, and groups of you will share in particular views of the events. Your own beliefs are moving in the direction of *The Reference Point* and this provides you with a healthy interpretation of what's going to happen. This will reduce the amount of fear and confusion during *The Revealing*. While others might be witness to a struggle, you'll be watching an incredible renewal of *Reality*, one that paints a world of wonders.

You might remember Aman from the previous book. Aman is concerned with the religious aspects of your experience. Many religions possess teachings that refer to 'end of the world' scenarios. If it helps you, *The Revealing* can be linked to those ideas. If it doesn't help, i would disregard these teachings. They aren't crucial to what's coming.

Aman has also asked me to share some ideas around those changes in your behaviour that have you acting seriously. As you notice yourself acting in this way, your surroundings will start to seem very special to you. Acting seriously won't simply be limited to your words and actions, anymore. Everything, including all the props within the setting, will start to seem important.

There is something valued in many religions; it's known as the sacred. The sacred is understood to place importance on some things, while labeling other things as common, or less important. When you begin acting seriously, there won't be any distinction for you between the sacred and the everyday. *Everything* will feel sacred. This is a positive step towards going *Home*, but only up to a point. You must be careful to *never* consider these things as actually real, or true. Their sacredness only lies in their ability to get you *Home*. Remember that we can't bring anything in Reality, *Home* with us. Don't get too attached to any of it. i hope this makes things clear.

The sacred places and moments, the acting seriously and the shared experiences with others will definitely increase your enjoyment of the journey *Home*. At times, they might even tempt you into staying a little longer. You'll be living your lifetime with greater fullness and intensity. Your experiences will feel very special, and there's a reason for this. If the process wasn't enjoyable, you might not choose to return to us. There needed to be an incentive for you to make this choice. The journey *Home* needed to be better than your previous experiences of *Reality*, or else you'd never want to leave. It's a tricky business this going *Home*, because it makes use of the thing you're leaving, to get you to leave it.

You aren't leaving anything.
You aren't going anywhere.

Because the beginning of *Reality* involved a willful act of pretending, you can start to consider the possibility that you aren't truthfully leaving anything you don't already possess. *The Gathering* refers to our loss from them as a kind of temporary, deep sleep. We've been under a spell, or enchantment.

10

In addition to feelings of relief and sacredness, you'll begin to enjoy wonder and gratitude. All four are related. Wonder comes with the sense of freshness, preparation for *The Revealing* offers. Everything seems new, again. Understanding the connection between *The Revealing* and going *Home* introduces us to gratitude. It will all seem worth it, the changes, the struggle and the responsibilities aren't meaningless anymore. There was a time when these things led you to feelings of despair and hopelessness. With an adjustment of our beliefs, we can interpret everything in a new way. Now, we find that we're headed somewhere. The 'somewhere' to which we're headed in *this* world is called *The Reference Point*. You've gathered this from the messages in the previous book and the title of this one. i've been mostly speaking about *Home* up until now, but since your traveling involves four-dimensional *Reality*, *The Reference Point* might be easier to imagine as a destination.

Home is beyond the experience of *Reality*.

Everyone understands what it feels like to work towards an achievable goal. You've all achieved things in *Reality*, as part of your programs. Part of what kept you moving in the direction of your goal was noticing that you were successfully completing all the little steps along the way. You could measure your progress in this way, and predict when you would eventually reach your goal, based on how long it took and *would take* you to complete those steps. One thing always leads to another, in *Reality*.

The others tend to judge us, based on our ability to reach our goals. Since 'the reaching of goals' is part of everyone's program and we all want to complete these programs, there's an encouragement factor that's automatically built-in to our relationship patterns. This factor was supposed to help us encourage the others, but somehow turned us into critics. The world began to place a value on whether or not someone achieved their goals. This value was then quickly connected to the person who possessed the goal and led to a valuing, or discrediting of that person. This hardly seems fair, given that most of us don't even remember what our actual program goals are, nor whether we can even realistically accomplish any goal we suspect might be related to that program.

We are judged on the results of a guessing game.

Guess who wins? Appearances tell us it's likely the ones who have interpreted the 'signs' correctly, or the ones who have been lucky enough to guess rightly in their choice of goals. In addition, we must also remember the indirect effects of our working towards any goal. These are difficult to rely on, as we hope for any success and respect among friends. There are better ways than relying on luck.

The goals related to our programs appear naturally for us. They always appear at the right time. Are you 'naturally' good at something? Is there something you're doing that results in words of encouragement from others? The others might even perform *acts* to encourage you, clearing the way for the success of your goals by removing any obstacles. These are the right goals, the goals from our program. Any other goals, are false goals. They either belong to other people, or they serve purposes that only help the few. Individuals who rally the support of others away from their own goals, often hope to keep us stuck within *their* vision of *Reality.* Their vision is not your vision. You'll recognize these false goals for what they are, and it's likely you haven't fallen for any of them in quite a while.

Perhaps it's not so difficult dealing with the opinions of others. We gradually learn to alter our beliefs enough, so that we perceive their comments as misguided. We begin to form new social circles that recognize the value in our goals, and we appreciate the resulting improvement in our sense of well-being. The trouble appears in the consistency of these efforts. Occasionally, we get sidetracked by self-doubt and make small judgements about ourselves. They're small and they don't always last, but they do happen. This is an unhelpful part of the world's conditioning that prompted *The Gathering* to reach out to you. This kind of self-judgement should have ended long ago. The ever-increasing pressures to 'be this,' or to 'do that,' while you're here, are interfering with the simplest parts of your programs. Because of self-doubt, our lifetimes always seem to be about someone else. For this reason, the plans for our lifetime don't ever seem good enough, so we try to copy someone else's plan. Follow in the direction of help and support during these moments.

Self-doubt can't last.

Aman often reminds me that every day is a kind of 'Judgement Day' in *Reality*. We don't really need the event of *The Revealing* to remind us of it, but it will seem to emphasize the differences, as we get closer to it. Judgements are based on incorrect perception. *The Reference Point* will guide us to correct perception. If we recognize the important difference as *The Reference Point* shows it to us, we don't *ever* have to go back to the experience of false perception. We won't ever feel the need to judge, again. The brain will still perform its functions of organizing and categorizing, but it won't be drawn to label someone or something as 'wrong.' To be 'wrong' implies that the thing or person isn't worthy of being. This perception is particularly false, given everyone's true value. *The Gathering* knows your worth. Knowing you, it can't see anything *other* than your worth. i'll help you to remember it.

11

**seek not in the questioning
but in a single answer**

**for in its presence
are all questions needless,
and forgotten**

Human lifetimes present so many unanswered questions. Realizing something of our true value apart from *Reality*, simplifies these questions and offers us some reassurance that everything will be as it was meant to be. The 'single answer' is the knowledge of who you really are. It will unlock all those answers for you. *The Revealing* will shine a light on this knowledge.

When a light is switched on, we immediately look. It's instinctive. We feel physically drawn to it. We crave sensual information, to enrich our experience. We might even run toward the sound of physical danger, or the smell of a burning fire. These reactions can be very beneficial, especially where rescue is needed. They can call us to action.

Stimulating the senses might also produce another reaction, depending on the type of person we believe we are. They can fill us with the information we've been craving and leave us feeling contented. Feeling full and satisfied, we could then follow a less active approach to what's happening. We could choose to watch. Of course, we're always ready to take action, when called upon. But, we'd rather wait for the right acting cues before doing anything.

It's not always important for us to act in *every* scene. It's fun to be the 'star of the show,' but it's not always our show. If it's not our place to act, we're more likely to interfere with the scene than help. We could be doing more harm than good. Supporting roles are just as important.

Have you ever felt that some things needed to happen, before other things could? This usually happens when we look back on our experiences. We notice a critical sequence of events had to take place, in order to produce a certain result. Sometimes, it was something we really wanted and we're glad things happened the way they did. Since we can only realize this afterwards, it's probably best not to assume that acting is always the best choice. Recognize the cues; wait for the call. If you're the only one there, it's your show. Offer help.

Understanding when, where and how to act grows with age and experience. We learn when to get involved and when not. We don't always need to wait for age and experience to teach us these things. i realized this many times, because i was the one who liked to ask for advice and cues during an emergency. Yes, i might have even begged for someone, anyone, to tell me what to do.

You don't need to beg.

Ask once. The answer you get will prompt you. There's no need to keep asking. The results aren't your responsibility. You might feel as if they are, because the situation is so emotionally intense. During *The Revealing*, the intensity of the experience is connected to the process, not the results. You might say that the process *always* leads to the results, because that's what you've been led to believe. This belief for *Reality* doesn't apply during *The Revealing*. It's temporarily tossed aside, so that *The Unexpected* can occur.

If it helps the scene, you can *act* confused about the strange results of what just happened. Just remember that you're acting, and that *The Revealing* is the reason why. You're able to do the same type of acting within *The Dreaming*. Unexpected results happen all the time, when we're dreaming. If they don't bother us there, why should they bother you here? *The Dreaming* is just another part of *Reality*. Let me reassure you. The surprise results in either case aren't telling you that something's wrong. They're surprising you so that you'll realize it's time to wake up. Weird dreams always used to wake me up at night. i enjoyed it, because waking-up made the dreams easier to remember.

12

It seems you're starting to wonder about all the confusion *The Revealing* is going to bring into the world. Yes, there will be confusion, but only at first. Many of us don't like the idea of change, especially when it's forced upon us. Change seems bad and unpleasant because we aren't certain of our future. We don't have faith in change, because it has let us down before. If we could only be sure that it would lead us to something good, we might be able to feel differently about it.

The type of change you're worried about is the one caused by other people. When it's caused by other people, *The Gathering* doesn't call it change; it calls it manipulation. Manipulation tries to change another person's program to match with theirs. The intentions seem good, but they're based on a limited vision of the future. The direct and indirect results of manipulation are always unreliable. *Real* change is a lot like allowing things to settle naturally, on their own and without interference. The kind of change connected with *The Revealing* isn't caused by anyone in *Reality*. If it was, there wouldn't be any room for *The Unexpected*. *The Revealing* is different. It will provide you with a glimpse of the good that it's doing, while it's making changes. This will give you confidence in its ways. It's also better, in that it doesn't force you to do anything. You're free to respond to it in any way you feel is helpful. If you aren't already there, *The Revealing* can take you straight to *The Reference Point*.

Let's start with you. If you can be the one person appearing calm while everything else is madness, you'll be able to help in *The Revealing*. Occasionally you'll be surprised by future changes; eventually, nothing will surprise you. If you're not surprised, you're not upset. If you don't seem worried, others take notice. You'll become like *The Unexpected* in those situations. You'll be doing the opposite of what others expect. People will notice that you're calm and they'll want to feel calm, too!

Calm realizes itself as personal strength.

The others will try to imitate you, even if they don't *really* understand why you're calm. The only thing they *do* understand in those moments, is that it seems the better option. In times of difficulty, we naturally seek peace. In moments of distress, we work to achieve balance by introducing its opposite. Calm eventually eases distress, and stabilizes the scene. Given your new perspective, if you can bring this kind of help, others will follow your lead. This will reduce the amount of damage.

Feeling grateful for your calm strength, the others will carry the direct and indirect effects of your performance into the future. You're helping to shape what's coming. i've told you what's on the way, but it hasn't quite taken its final shape. We can't stop it from coming, but we *can* adjust to how it will appear. In these times, we like to enjoy the way things look, so we alter parts of *Reality* to get the results we want. Why not apply that same approach to *The Revealing*? Accepting that change doesn't have to be bad, we can shape it in a new way, a way that looks good for us. We shape it through our perceptual beliefs. You're doing it now.

Practicing the use of calm strength might feel exhausting, at first. Yes, it's possible to get tired from acting calm. The reasons behind this have to do with our resistance to the calm behaviours. We aren't completely practiced in using them. Our physical and emotional habits are pretty well established at an early age, and it takes a bit of effort readjusting them. Effort meets resistance, which leads to fatigue. Eventually, you'll get tired of making yourself tired and remove the part about resisting. No resistance means no effort, which results in less fatigue and more happiness. Removing resistance, saves time.

Saving time, shortens time.

Achieving a state of calm feels like a kind of surrender. We let go of the resistance and surrender to calm. Calm is not our enemy, so it's okay to surrender to it. But, calm has been described in ways that are false. Some feel it's a sign of laziness, an unintelligent personality, or an uncaring attitude. Feelings of jealousy might even be found in regard to calm demonstrations, in the sense that the calm person might consider themselves 'better' than others, or above their concerns. The calm person appears mysterious and misunderstood.

When we surrender to calm, we receive a bonus effect from it. The extra benefit is trust. It doesn't come from the calm itself, but from the removal of resistance. Surrendering rebuilds trust. It doesn't do it all at once, only a little at a time. This is because resistance is rarely removed 'all at once.' If we start to decrease the resistance to something, we begin to gradually receive the thing we kept away. It returns to us. There was a time when we welcomed many things and people, so we can accept that we once *did* welcome it. That's why i used the word 'return.' If we once welcomed them, it was because we trusted they had value. They didn't even need to be personally valuable, they just seemed worth welcoming.

Without realizing it, our decision to reduce the amount of resistance in our lives brings back the benefits of trust. We were initially hoping to lessen our fatigue, but soon noticed that something else was happening. As this feeling of trust began returning, it didn't really feel connected with anything specific. It was more of a general feeling of trust that grew. The sensation was enjoyable and further encouraged the release of resistance, *all* resistance. This is no accident. *The Gathering* knows about the connection between surrender, trust and calm. It sees this connection as being important to your future. Eventually all resistance must be surrendered, regaining *full* trust and returning *Home*. Don't worry, you won't have to do all the work. You only need to do the job of reaching *The Reference Point*. The final part about 'complete surrender' will happen on its own. *The Gathering* understands that there are no complete experiences in *Reality*, so it doesn't expect you to be able to achieve something you can't imagine. The closest you can imagine yourself getting to it, is *The Reference Point*.

13

When i discussed the idea of perceived sounds during *The Revealing*, i used the idea of stagehands making adjustments and preparations for upcoming scenes and activities. i'm now going to substitute the word 'stagehands' for 'helpers.' It's not a big switch, so it shouldn't lead to any confusion. You might even like the new word better.

Helpers are everywhere and in every moment. They aren't actual people, but they *can* sometimes take-on the appearance of people. This enables them to be more efficient, while also keeping their nature hidden. For the most part, they are invisible to us. This will change. *The Revealing* likes to show us things, and one of the things it's about to show us are the helpers. In order to prepare you for their appearance, i'd like to ask that you use your imagination to connect with your beliefs about the title 'helpers.' Do you have any concerns about invisible helpers? How do you imagine you would *feel* if you encountered one of them? What do they look like to you? How do they speak, or communicate? Admitting these things to yourself *now*, will get you ready.

In time, you'll discover whether your assumptions about the helpers were correct. You might even be pleasantly surprised about a few things. When you encounter the helpers, do not assist them unless you're asked. You should encourage them in their work. Helpers can do things humans can't. This is because of their function in *Reality*. They don't need to be bound by time or space, as we do. They can appear and disappear as needed. When they *do* disappear, it's not necessarily an indication that they've gone somewhere else. It's more likely that they've gone 'somewhen' else, in the same spot. They do this to get things ready for what's about to happen next, and to tidy up what was left behind.

Helpers have full access within *all* areas of *Reality*, including *The Dreaming* and *The Dimensions of the Dead*. They receive their instructions from *Reality*, itself. Because of this, they are single-minded. They're only focused on their work. It's possible to communicate with them, but the messages must be sent quickly and directly. You may get a response to your message, or you may not. If you don't get an answer, it's because they haven't any answer to give you. Please don't be offended. They are helpful, but not 'polite' or 'friendly' in ways valued by humans.

Helpers have a limited capacity for memory. They operate from moment to moment. If you interact with a certain helper and then encounter them again, it's doubtful they will recognize you from that previous occasion. Aside from their short memory, the lack of personal recognition from them is due to the fact that you always look the same. Whether you're two or ninety-two, you'll look to *them* as a mixture of all the ways you have ever appeared and *will* ever appear, in your lifetime. To them you're always the same person. You never change. If the helpers *could* appreciate the way everyone grows and changes, it would end up being a terrible distraction for them. It's better this way.

Learning about helpers may lead you to wondering if you could ask them about your future, or about your lost keys. i've tried several times over the years, but they simply don't understand the questions. We see them popping in and out of the scene, doing their work, but they don't even realize they're moving through time. Their activities just seem to flow, one to the next. As they perform one activity, they've already forgotten the previous one.

The instructions they receive from *Reality* are similar to 'do this,' or 'move that.' They don't get to choose what to do, nor do they get to decide *how* it should be done. Because of their limited memory, they don't really learn anything as they work. They are preprogrammed for certain tasks, and those are the tasks they complete. They lack the ability to reason 'why' they do, what they do. To ask them a 'why' question will only lead to your frustration.

Helpers don't feel frustrated, they simply help.

Many times, people will begin to feel that the helpers aren't doing things very efficiently. The human perspective only allows us to imagine the near effects of the helpers' efforts. The effects of what the helpers are doing is often beyond our narrow vision. Since the helpers can't take anyone's suggestions for doing their work, it's probably best to trust that they are doing the right thing. If you alter what a helper has done, they will simply return to correct it, as many times as needed. They never get tired.

Never worry that you might physically bump into a helper, or vice versa. Their bodies aren't solid in the way of our bodies. Although you'll soon begin to recognize them, they will seem to be made up of the substances closest to them. For example, if you see them in midair, they'll appear to be made of air particles, and so on. Appearing to be made of air particles, you can easily pass through them without their notice. Helpers don't need to eat, drink or breathe, as we do. If you notice them underwater, they're perfectly safe. They don't suffer physical damage, or sickness.

Noticing the presence of the helpers reminds you that you're never, truly alone. This will become obvious to you. It'll be so clear in fact, that you'll move past the idea of feeling the need to believe in it. *The Revealing* has a way of taking you beyond belief. It won't take you all the way to knowledge, but it can inspire confidence.

As mentioned, you may be asked to assist the helpers. The need for this comes from *Reality's* current inability to keep up with the many requests for changes. It only has so many helpers. When you are called to assist, simply do as you are asked. Please do it quickly. There's no time for discussion about it, and you generally don't need to know why. You will not be thanked.

Helping, is its own reward.

You can't call upon helpers. They don't work for anyone, specifically. If you're in trouble, call for other people. Helpers are there for the situation, not the person. When people respond to your call for rescue, the helpers make sure the responders have the tools they need to assist you.

The other reason you're unable to call the helpers is because they don't have names. Having a name makes you identifiable in time and space. Once people learn your name, they can place you. Helpers have no real place. They serve a function.

Luckily, there are plenty of other invisibles who are different from the helpers. *The Revealing* won't make these other beings visible to you. The invisibles have come to assist you and the others, in reaching *The Reference Point*. They've already been where you're going and have come back to assist with *The Revealing,* instead of going straight *Home.* If one of them should happen to tell you their name, you may use it to call upon them for assistance. They will always be nearby. The invisibles will help as guides. They can keep you traveling in the right direction by teaching you the right habits for your goal. When i use the word 'direction' it has more to do with your choices and actions, than a direction on a map of the Earth. The journey to *The Reference Point* isn't one of great, physical distance. You won't need your passport. The invisibles will help you with hints, and clues in many forms. Keep your senses ready. They won't make personal choices for you.

Many of you will be surprised to find that you're able to happily reach *The Reference Point* without any actual direction from the invisibles. This will probably be the case for you. i hope you're not too disappointed. Sometimes it's enough to know that they're around, if you need them.

14

Let's put aside those notions of traveling and direction for a few moments. i'm worried they might be giving you the wrong impression. Achieving *The Reference Point* is about becoming a certain kind of person. It's not based on looking like this person, but upon ways of acting, believing, and feeling. You might understand these characteristics to be 'inside' you, for now. *The Revealing* will shift much of what's 'inside' and place it on the 'outside.' Without preparation, the things we hold inside will do a lot of damage when they suddenly move out into the world. Once they're out, we can't control their effects any longer.

Thankfully, the items that will cause damage don't tend to accumulate inside us. The body doesn't like to keep them and has no place to put them. They are reactive in the moment and then quickly dissolve. They don't cause too many problems because they don't interact with the outside world. By preparing for those moments before *The Revealing* comes, we can prevent them. No reaction from inside means no disaster outside. It's seems pretty simple, but there's more.

You aren't aware of them, when they happen.

They don't appear in the *attention space* now and *The Revealing* won't be warning us about them later. If we didn't prepare ahead of time, a lot of the witnessed damage and destruction would unfold, without understanding where or how they originated. Not knowing where something comes from, or its cause, leaves us feeling helpless to stop the destruction and prevent further damage. The causes and events would appear random.

We possess a certain kind of power that lies hidden from us, just below the surface of the *attention space*. In coming to *Reality*, we limit ourselves for the purposes of this experience. Even though we make ourselves 'smaller' for an earthly existence, the power is still secretly with us. It's like having a buried treasure you can't tell anyone about, because you've forgotten where you've hidden it. The power has an intelligence to it, and is very active within us. It's activities are based on truth and naturally conflict with those of *Reality*, which hinges on illusion, hence the potential for destruction. Your hidden strength wants to correct the lies, *all* of them at once. Without getting ready, this point will become very clear for us in *The Revealing*. The way we prepare is by gradually bringing our perception closer to truth. If we're close to the truth when the truth comes out, our 'inside world' won't disagree with the 'outside world.' Combining things which are in agreement doesn't cause much damage, but introducing elements antagonistic could be catastrophic. Combining similar elements can also work to enhance, or improve a situation.

Many of you will reach *The Reference Point* before *The Revealing* comes. You will have completed the needed preparations and confusion will be kept to a minimum. Your efforts are so important, and very much appreciated by the rest of us. i wish i could give you a clear idea of the value of your work, but *Reality* doesn't offer any way for me to do so. As we continue with the preparations, you have a choice of two options. You can choose to complete your existing program, or to focus on *Home*. In your case, your program already includes the option to return *Home*. If you choose *Home*, you're not making a mess of your program. The *Home* option is what led us to you at the start of the first book. *The Gathering* knew that those of you who were equipped with this option, would be easier to reach. Once contacted, you would later influence the rest of the population.

15

You're destined for *The Reference Point*. You're becoming a *person* of *The Reference Point*. Once you become that person, you will belong with *The Reference Point*. With that connection, you'll experience a sense of being 'more' than your person. You'll have benefits and options available to you, that only seemed imaginary up to then. This enhancement comes from combining similar elements. You'll reach *The Reference Point* because you'll be similar to it.

Getting yourself ready will involve something called the 'quest,' or 'rite of passage' experience. Once a person reaches a certain age, they often go searching for themselves. It's considered a very meaningful step towards personal happiness. The ways for finding your Self can be as personal as you like. There doesn't seem to be only one way of finding it. We can make the process as simple or as complicated as we want, but we must practice it consistently. If we keep changing the plan and starting over, we won't achieve much success. People like to change their plan when they feel that another plan seems better. When practiced consistently, *all* plans for finding your Self are equally effective.

People start wanting to find their Self because of questions. Questions guide the process. The person starts feeling a bit lost and uncertain. Many things appear to have changed for them, and the old ways of doing and looking at things aren't working any longer. They can't seem to reach the things and relationships they want from this lifetime.

Looking for answers leads to those answers.

The answers aren't always clear at first, and may lead to more questions, but you *can* find them in *Reality*. As mentioned, all you need to get started are the questions. Look to others as you begin searching, they can be a fun source of information. They enjoy answering your questions, it makes them feel intelligent and helpful. Asking others socializes the process and saves time. We also enjoy answering our *own* questions for similar reasons. Remember that it's good to have many answers for each question. Gather several answers before deciding on the right answer to your question. The best ones tend to be a combination of answers that match with your character traits and beliefs about the world.

The question related to the 'one answer' in chapter 11 is the question of who you are. When people go searching for themselves, if it's not a search for purpose, it's ultimately one of identity. Something within you realizes that you are *not* this person. If you're not this person, then who *are* you? *Reality* will never tell you outright, but it can offer you some clues. Putting the clues together places you firmly on the road to solving the mystery. Groups of hints and gathered evidence will start to form a pattern. Combining patterns builds images within your imagination. In time, the images will tell a story. Stories can tell us about something, without naming the thing, itself. The story you hear will be *about* you, but it will not be you. Unfortunately, that's as close as *Reality* can bring you. You are more than your story.

Reality won't tell you who you are, but *The Revealing* can.

The Revealing won't last. While it's here, you'll discover things *Reality* can't teach you. It will be a temporary 'window,' or 'doorway' into which we will look to find some of the answers to our many questions. The answers will be helpful.

One day, you might find yourself at a point where you believe you know who you are. You will be incorrect. This statement might tempt you to feel discouraged about your search. In the moment you realized your conclusions were false, you approached the truth. That feeling of finally 'finding your Self' is more accurately called satisfaction. It's different from knowing. Satisfaction is the reward for all your hard work. It will last a short while and then new questions will appear. You'll welcome them and resume the search.

Finally, all of the searching teaches us that there is no one else left to be, other than our Self. Getting acquainted with it means letting it be who it is, and allowing your Self to be who *you* are. You are an original. You are your Self.

16

The Revealing will alter your perception of time.

Please remember that when i use the word 'time,' i'm also talking about space. They are in combination. *Reality* doesn't like to admit it, but time is also elastic. We can stretch it out and shorten it, as needed. It appears to move in one of two directions for us. We can move forward in time, or backward. Both ways of moving are done through perception. We receive information through our physical senses, compare it with the information we have and decide if we're moving forward, backward, speeding up, or slowing down. In most cases, we feel that we are moving forward and that it's the only option we have. Time seems to have some control over us.

The feeling is undeniable, and yet we can sometimes be taken back in time, or held momentarily 'outside' of time. Certain smells, sounds or places can trigger these experiences. Exceptions to time offer us the possibility for one day regaining control over it. If time *was* in complete control, we wouldn't have had these experiences. These unusual moments allow us to appreciate that *Reality* has some natural flaws in the way it works.

Reality is running out of time.

More specifically, it's running out of one type of time, called linear time. Linear time is the kind that moves in one direction from a starting point. Even though we perceive that time can also move in reverse, through memories and imagination, *Reality* focuses on the forward-moving option.

Linear time is the easiest model of time for helping us complete our lifetimes. Like a story, it's based on beginnings and endings.

The Revealing will introduce episodes of non-linear time. This is because linear time is incompatible with the truth. Non-linear time doesn't really feel like time at all. It has no real beginning or end. It happens all at once. Since the human brain can't process the whole thing at once, *The Revealing* will be showing you a series of visual pictures. This helps to organize non-linear time in ways we can appreciate, before it's gone. The series of pictures themselves, will also be non-linear. They will be organized by subject, theme or any number of other ways. Regardless of how they're grouped, they will always be for your benefit because you are the one receiving them. The non-linear moments are personal.

In some ways, the world's visual artists have been preparing you for this. Some filmmakers actually realized they were getting you ready, while others did not. As soon as they began editing the film production process, they were learning to manipulate time. They were playing with images to produce *virtual* shifts in time and place. These 'jumps' or 'cuts' trained you to accept that people could move around in time, according to a reasonable plan. You could accept these breaks in the rule of time and assemble them with your imagination, to receive a coherent message. You accepted that the visual shifts in time weren't real, so they didn't upset you.

Using this model of the film industry, *The Revealing* is going to turn your perception into a kind of 'movie projector.' As i said in chapter 14, *The Revealing* will be allowing us to experience what's 'inside' us as being 'outside' of us. One of the ways it will do this in connection with non-linear time, is to get us to project the inside, non-linear images onto our own perceptual 'movie screen.' These particular images will appear to be outside of us.

They are not. *Reality* can't reproduce them quickly enough in the outside world, no matter how hard the helpers try. Instead, the quick, non-linear images will be projected onto the *attention space*.

You have a light in you that allows you to produce images for yourself. This isn't news. It's the same light that powers the images of your dreams and imagination. When you close your eyelids, you're still able to visualize things. The images have a different quality than the images gathered from the outside world, but you can still appreciate them. Without this light, visual perception couldn't exist.

Linear time is a series of images connected together in a row. Each image represents a moment of time. If we connect each image together in a series, and quickly look at them, we get an impression of movement within those images. This is similar to how movies work. If we look at each image separately, we feel no sense of movement and therefore, no time appears to pass for the characters in the image. Linear time appears to have stopped, or disappeared. Looking at a series of images at a certain speed, produces the effect of movement for those characters in the image. The image doesn't appear to move at that point, just the items within the image. Becoming focused on their movements, we begin to forget we're looking at an image. The activities become the priority for our visual senses. We can speed up the movement of the images or slow them down, but we usually prefer a steady speed to those passing moments. Adjusting the speed would either give us the impression of time speeding up, or slowing down.

If we find ourselves in a quiet place, without much activity, we will feel that linear time slows down. This is relaxing for many of us. The rest prefer the busier environments, filled with lots of activity. There, they find that time passes quickly and this feeling produces a kind of emotional excitement. If we place a person within the experience opposite to what they enjoy, the effects of time will be the same, but the enjoyment will be missing.

Time is connected with perception.

We can't separate time and perception, while we're here. Luckily, perception is open to all forms of time. This will allow *The Revealing* to use your perception to show you many things. Feel like you want to read this chapter again?

17

Images from non-linear time will include alternate lifetime possibilities. They aren't in focus, as you live this lifetime. *The Revealing* will show you images of things that 'never happened,' as far as your memories are concerned. These other possibilities are based on the choices you made in this lifetime, as well as the ones you considered making. In the hopes of keeping you entertained, *Reality* tries to prepare for all possibilities. It does this by creating *other*, linear timelines based on these choices. We aren't aware of them because our perception is limited to showing us only one timeline. Part of your Self is alive in those timelines, too. Those other versions of you aren't quite the same as this you, because they only exist in possibility. They are virtual versions of you that provide *Reality* with information helpful for customer service. Learning all it can about your person, helps *Reality* provide for your stay. Those kinds of details matter to it.
The images from non-linear time will contain people, places

and objects from this lifetime, but they will seem different in many ways. Because your lifetime is linked with those of many others, the other timelines will also be based on decisions *they* made, or didn't make. The variations for possible timelines is incredible, but they're all here. Somehow, *Reality* has managed to assemble them all and *The Revealing* has access to them. Soon, you will too.

Witnessing things through non-linear time will offer you the chance to look at your character in new ways. Humans tend to repeat their behaviours. We form habits, for the sake of convenience. When the habits stay too long, we don't consider that there could be other ways of doing things. *The Revealing* will show you times when you *did* do things differently, and how things turned out. It will show you both good and bad outcomes. Both are helpful in informing us about the future. They show us whom to embrace and what to avoid. This information will allow you to break old habits and start new ones. It's never too late to correct ourselves.

Given access to non-linear time, you might experience a 'jump' into one of those other timelines. This happens when we focus too intently on them. We draw ourselves into them by wanting. We see something we like and chase after it. It's an automatic, human response. If this should happen to you, the experience won't last. The other timeline will be disrupted by your being there, and the helpers will bring you back. You might feel saddened by this. Trust me, you're better off in your own timeline.

You're important to us, here.

The Revealing is capable of showing you images from other lifetimes, too. This will only happen in special situations. The images from non-linear time need to be understood by the person watching them. If you aren't capable of understanding them, they won't appear for you.

They will be in your scope of vision, but your perception won't be able to grasp them in any meaningful way. You'll skip over those images automatically, and focus on the ones you recognize. This lifetime is the important one.

Time has much to offer us. Your beliefs about time will guide your experience of it. While you're in *Reality*, moments of time can be opportunities for generosity. We like to share gifts with others and these can be given in many ways. The more valued of these are received as the moments we share with others. Moments don't last, but the memories of them do. That's why they're appreciated. Everything else will eventually be repurposed for the sake of *Reality* and its future guests. Remember this while you're in those moments, and watch what happens.

18

Patience is valuable, as we wait for the arrival of *The Revealing*. It can't be rushed. Even though you've learned a lot about it and feel ready for it to come now, its appearance needs to be unexpected. It needs to sneak-in to *Reality*.

Some of the factors that guide its surprise arrival are related to your program, your choices, and your resistance to it. Because it has a personal element to it, it will appear both generally *and* individually. For some, the two will happen in the same moment. For others, there will be a slight delay between those moments. Eventually, it will come to everyone. i'm helping with both forms of arrival, and so are you.

Now that you understand a bit more about time, you might be considering ways of skipping ahead to *The Revealing's* appearance. If you would like to shorten the time before it comes, a good way to do so would be to focus on reaching *The Reference Point*. This will keep you busy and focused on other things, trusting that it will come when it comes. Focusing on an unexpected desire, can lead to a feeling of time slowing down. This can reduce any hope we might have, for its arrival. Distract yourself in the right way, a way that indirectly prepares you for *The Revealing*.

You have many times shown great patience in waiting. This situation is no different from those and it will reward your patience in surprising ways. Unknown elements of *The Revealing's* arrival might cause some to worry, and the 'unknowns' then make it harder for them to wait. Worrying too much about *The Revealing* can also start to produce unspoken feelings of fear around its coming. If we don't talk about the fear before then, fear will be released in the form of terror.

Fear is one of those 'inside' things the body can store. Fear is produced *in* the body, so the body has ways of temporarily holding onto it. Fear is produced by us, *not* the body. The body can't really get rid of it without our help. We're responsible for its production, management and disposal. We should arrange for this before *The Revealing* comes.

There are many ways of doing this. You are doing one of them, now. You're informing yourself about *The Revealing*. The great majority of human fears seem to be connected with the 'unknown.' The more we learn about something, the less of a mystery it becomes. The unknown gradually becomes familiar to us. This lets the specific fear out of the body, or transforms it into confidence. Your body prefers to store confidence.

Another option for reducing or eliminating fear relates to working *with* fear. Fear has proven useful over time as a means for personal protection. But, many of us have allowed fear to take control of us. It's good at what it does. It can still protect your person. Working *with* fear allows you to maintain control, while allowing aspects of fear to do their job. Sometimes you need the boost of physical energy and the quick reflexes to complete your part, during a scene. Fear supports you in those situations. At this stage, you are able to recognize when the feeling of fear is growing within you. Depending on your acting needs, choose the parts of fear that will help you get the job done. When we select certain parts of something for use, there's a better chance of staying in charge. Understanding that we're able to do this, lets us realize we're no longer at the mercy of fear.

Fear has had its influence over people for a very long time. It has become a kind of 'force' against which we feel the need to struggle. Originally designed as a helping influence for preservation and extreme emotional responses in acting, it has become the great limiting factor of our age. It discourages and prevents us from doing what we need to do, to complete our programs. Fear has become a kind of 'default' response for many of our challenges.

It would be correct to also say that certain fearful experiences are enjoyed by many people. They have discovered a way of working *with* fear for the purposes of entertainment. On some level, they've learned to feel certain parts of fear without becoming afraid. They've figured out how to disregard the parts of fear that allow it to control us. Fear doesn't mind this, at all. It never really wanted the control anyway.

Should you encounter a person who has become afraid, tell them you are here to help them. Ask them to describe the fear for you. Select the different elements of their experience and give each one another name. You may choose names like 'excited,' 'tired,' 'angry,' 'hurt,' and so on. These will distract them from a focus on fear, and help to clarify their perception.   If the person is willing to accept the new names as appropriate to their experience, they will begin to reconnect with their self-control. You'll notice the change right away. Patiently, wait with them until they seem calm.

19

Whether you like it or not, you will experience certain things during *The Revealing* that *need* to happen. When they present themselves, you will quickly move through a combination of emotions. You will feel as if there was no choice in their coming. Once they've passed, any sensations of disruption will leave you and you'll be able to decide if the experiences proved helpful. The experiences won't last long.

We don't always choose what's best for us.

During *The Revealing*, you will also understand that there won't be many opportunities for you to stop and rest. You've encountered similar situations during this lifetime, when you understood that rest wouldn't come until the experience was over. *The Revealing* will be similar to those situations in that you will find rest at the end of the experience. Thankfully, due to the effect of non-linear time, not much linear time will have actually passed. You'll be surprised to discover this. Similar to those brief morning dreams which seemed so much longer in your remembering, the experience will only take you through a brief section of linear time.

Your perception is able to function at a much faster rate than that of your physical body's movements. We tend to estimate our abilities based on how fast the body can accomplish them. For example, your pace for 'silent' reading is much quicker than the speed at which you normally speak. The non-linear portions of *The Revealing* will be geared for perception only, and will not make you tired. They might however, leave you feeling hungry. These perceptual episodes will likely produce a feeling of being energized, or excited. You can use this residual feeling of energy toward any physical activities that will later involve the body. The 'energized' feeling won't last, and the body should then be given rest.

It's possible that during *The Revealing*, you won't even stop to consider the need for rest. You'll be far too busy. Your perceptual focus will be away from the needs of your body, and more attentive to the information you're receiving. The body will wait for you as you go through this process. If it needs anything, it will alert you when you return to your focus on this world.

Rest is different from peace.

As mentioned in the first book, rest is only needed for the physical body. Peace is not attainable in *Reality*, but we *can* experience something similar to it and call it peacefulness. You're all aware of peacefulness and you each have your own recipes for generating this feeling. You do things 'outside' to promote those enjoyable feelings 'inside.' i'm about to ask you to reverse this. It's not that you're doing things incorrectly, because they *do* seem to work for you. i'm just offering you another way.

Your inner and outer worlds are connected. They work together. Because we're focused on the 'outer' most of the time, we tend to give it more importance. Nothing else gets our attention in quite the same way. Something else will. It will be so impressive that we'll quickly forget all about the outside world. *The Revealing* will reacquaint us with the inside world. This inner world was once very important to us, so it won't seem foreign. In some ways, it might feel even *more* familiar to us than the outer world. It's because we were there first.

You've lived many lifetimes, and all of them began first, from within. Many of the things you encounter in the outside world start out as ideas. You understand this. Ideas begin 'inside' us. Whether they come from the imagination, or some other source, we eventually begin to picture them on the *attention space*. Once the picture gets clearer and better-defined, we start the process of transferring the idea into physical form. Humans believe that they can enjoy ideas, but only up to a point. Beyond that, we feel the need to put together a representation of our idea in *Reality*. Of course, it won't be the idea itself, but we can still enjoy using and having the model of it.

Turning our focus inward, we can begin to accept that we don't always need to have a physical model of our ideas, in order to enjoy them. It was only our preoccupation with the outside world that made us believe it. Ideas can be explored and discovered in ways within, that could never be attempted in a physical way. Ideas can grow, but once the model has been made, it will stay the way it is. A model is also limited in its production by available materials and techniques. Ever felt as though the book was better than the movie?

We each carry the idea of peace within us. We've tried to translate it in a physical way and found an acceptable experience in peacefulness. You've done well. It has made *Reality* far more enjoyable. If you're still interested in peace, let's visit the idea of it together. If you want, you can close your eyes before the visit. Begin by turning your attention to the place you keep your ideas. Find where you've stored the idea of peace. Open its container, remove it and imagine holding it. Stay with the idea of peace for a few moments and watch what happens. You'll simply be watching and adjusting to the idea, as you watch. When you feel ready, you can turn your attention somewhere else, while continuing to hold the idea of peace. You don't need to return it to storage.

As you focus on an idea, adjustments will begin to happen in both worlds. Because inner and outer are connected, your focus on one will affect the other. Was there a change in feeling, or perception, while you focused on peace? Did the physical body respond in some way, as a reaction to the activity? Do your surroundings somehow seem different from before the activity? Regardless of what may appear in *The Revealing*, peace is available to you as the idea of peace. Bringing it out of storage and keeping it handy, means that you can focus on it quickly and presently. You don't even need to wait for *The Revealing*. The world already provides you with plenty of occasions for calling upon peace. Turning to the idea also means that you won't have to wait for peace, or for peaceful conditions. You can have it now. The experience of *The Revealing* can be a peaceful one.

The *attention space* always has room for peace.

Ideas are one of the few things that truly belong to us. Descriptions of them can be shared, but until another person has access to your *attention space*, they won't be able to clearly appreciate the beauty of your ideas. Without access and permission, no one can take these ideas. They remain secure. No one can take your peace.

20

Enter the Witness spoke of the return of *Word*. It was during chapter 24. As more and more of you reach *The Reference Point*, the combination of arrivals will call *Word* into *Reality*. You won't be physically calling for it, but *Word* will notice all of you and see that its time has finally come. It's been waiting for enough of you to reach a certain level of perception, so that you could appreciate its presence. There were many times in history when humanity came close to the needed number, but because lifetimes were often shorter in length, it could never introduce itself.

Word is not the same as *The Revealing*. They are similar, but one is focused on a certain timing while the other watches for the welcoming effect of personal numbers. *Word* can arrive any time, even multiple times, but *The Revealing* will only happen once. *Word* doesn't use non-linear time in the way *The Revealing* does, though it *can* be used to decrease the amount of time needed to accomplish certain things. While *The Revealing* will make use of your current perceptual abilities, *Word* will expand upon them. The expansion will last as long as *Word* is present. Once humanity loses the critical number of people needed for its presence, *Word* will leave and so will the expansion of perception. *Reality* doesn't mind if *Word* comes, because the hope of *Word's* coming encourages people to stay longer in *Reality*. *Word* doesn't need to sneak in to *Reality*, it doesn't depend on *The Unexpected*.

Word operates on the principle of having common beliefs and interpretation, which lead to a grouping of perception.

When enough of us have a shared perception, *Word* can visit that perceptual 'room' of sharing and stay there. It can only visit if the 'room' is big enough. *Word* won't arrive 'empty handed.' Being present within your shared perception, means that you and the others will have full access to *Word* itself, and this includes all of its abilities. You won't be able to use *Word's* abilities individually, only together, as a group. It works with shared, or common goals, plans that benefit everyone. In its own way, experiencing *Word* is like belonging to a smaller version of *The Gathering*.

If you are within this grouping when it comes, you'll have two kinds of perception available to you. You'll be able to perceive things as an individual *and* as a group. You will be in contact with your *Word* group at all times and in all places. The group will only have access to the shared parts of your perception. The others won't be aware of any personal information. You might never physically meet any of the group's members during your lifetime. This won't bother you. You'll feel as close to them as if you *had* met them. *Where* the group's members are, isn't as important as what they share.

Word isn't really compatible with opposites. It's focused on the things we have in common. *Word* seeks agreement in all things. *Reality* is filled with differences. They're easy to find, and can distract us from the things we have in common. *The Reference Point* provides us with the right kind of perception for welcoming *Word*. There are many other types of shared perception in the world, but they never seem to grow beyond a certain point. Not enough people want to join them. *The Reference Point* gets us ready individually, but our decision to share in this way of perceiving, invites *Word*. Actually, it isn't much of a choice. *Reference Point* perception natural wants to share itself. This saves you the task of having to locate others, with whom to share it.

In connection with *Word*, your group won't notice any difference between the group and *Word*, itself. They will appear to be the same thing. *Word* will never try to take control of the group. Seeking agreement, it sees itself as an equal member. Unique in the abilities it brings, it also recognizes that each member brings their own special skills to the group. The group's power is shared within the group, as a group. The abilities don't stay within the group, however. They tend to have an effect on the outside world.

Sometimes the members of the group will notice that the group is having an effect on the world. They won't remember making any decisions about taking action in this way. The *Word* group doesn't make decisions because decisions are based on individual opinions. *Word,* through its abilities and by its nature, affects change just by being itself. It doesn't need to *do* anything. Still, things will happen because it's here.

Thankfully, *Word* brings us together. It doesn't notice our differences, only what we share. It sees us all as being in agreement. It increases our ability to recognize what we have in common with each other. Ignoring the differences allows us to accomplish things more quickly. Conflict is reduced. This is how *Word* saves time. The things with which we agree, are those that serve to benefit all of us and the world. We will have personal opinions and ideas about what's best for humanity, but alone, these ideas hold no power apart from *Word*.

21

All things and people interact, but they don't always work together. People can either choose for, or against. We can't successfully have both. The reasons for choosing to work together will secretly struggle against your original purposes for coming into *Reality*. You came to experience the differences. You *wanted* to enjoy moments of separation from everything and everyone. Forming groups and working together, naturally resist the purpose of *Reality*. Still, we can't deny that urge to reach out to others. On a very deep level, we accept that happiness is related to our being and working together. *Reality* accepts this and tries to arrange a kind of 'togetherness' based on the idea of our acting together within a continuing drama. It's hoping that occasions to pretend will be enough to satisfy your desire to be with one another, while still holding on to the idea of being separate individuals. Sometimes it works, many times it doesn't. We can't seem to stay away from each other, and so many of us are organizing for the common good. *Reality* will not interfere with what's happening, as long as you're happy, and as long as you continue to believe that *Reality* is your home.

Reality is very busy and doesn't always pay close attention. It won't notice certain things. For instance, it can't really recognize the difference between someone who realizes they're acting, and someone who doesn't. This gives us an opportunity. We can quietly play along in *Reality's* drama, while working towards our goal of returning *Home*. Performing in the drama also serves to satisfy the designs of our programs. This further reassures *Reality*. As far as *Reality* is concerned, you're simply reading a book and have no idea of yourself as an actor. It overlooks these things.

The Revealing will be something else, altogether. *Reality* will take notice, but it won't be able to do much about it. By then, it will be too late. The *only* thing *Reality* can do is react to the way things turn out. *The Revealing* will be a surprise to *Reality* and because of nonlinear time, it will appear to have quickly come and gone. The helpers will be in a momentary state of shock, as they wait for *Reality* to tell them what to do. *Reality* will quickly respond, but it won't be able to undo what *The Revealing* has accomplished. *Reality* won't be able to take away your experience of it, nor reverse the effects it's had upon your perception.

Reality doesn't understand that you're preparing yourself for *The Revealing*. It won't be able to see that you're one of the ones who will eventually be helping, in a state of calm awareness that all will be well. Regardless of how you decide to act in the coming days, *Reality* will never suspect that you can tell the difference between real and pretend.

Article 5

Your person, the others and your Self.

22

Bax here. *The Gathering* finds it strange to consider the idea of your person, the others and your Self as being separate topics for discussion. They know about individual identities, but they can't imagine them being apart from one another. Thankfully, i remember what it's like to spend time in *Reality*, and to experience the world as a person. i can appreciate how things look, when they've been temporarily disconnected from one another. Working with *Reality's* view of who we are will make it easier for me to help you understand the effects of what happened, when you decided to become a person. Before we start, i'd like to spend a few moments telling you about what happened to me after disappearing from the first book.

Before we started delivering those earlier messages, *The Gathering* decided that we would only share certain pieces of information with you. We had to be selective about what we said. You wouldn't need to know *everything* about *Reality*, only the parts that would get you *Home*. Finding the information was simple. All the important facts about *Reality* and how it works, exist at the *halfway point*. It's very near the area where you both enter *Reality* and return from your experience of a lifetime. As we approach the *halfway point*, the information becomes freely available, but viewing it can sometimes lead to our falling into *Reality*. i wanted to avoid falling, for as long as i could. No one enters *Reality* by accident, so it's not as if they're actually falling. It's a choice.

Viewing *Reality* from the *halfway point* offered me clear access to the information we needed, but there was a chance that i might end up choosing to enter *Reality* before the transfer process was complete. It's easy for individuals to be distracted by *Reality*. Thankfully, my wanting to deliver the message turned out to be stronger than my desire for *Reality*. A big part of my being able to stay focused was related to knowing that i would eventually be visiting the world anyway. There was no need to rush; i could stay as long as i wanted.

The *halfway point* is an interesting place. Being there feels a lot like waiting. It's just like that feeling people get, when they're about to make a choice. It's a mixture of wanting to go forward, and wanting to hold back.

Once the original message was delivered to you, *The Gathering* could then personalize the rest of it. i would enter *Reality* and collect the missing pieces of information, needed to get you *Home*. Sorry for not announcing that i was on my way. Things always happen instantly with *The Gathering*. There was basically 'no time' to tell you.

At last, we could be together.

My visits to *Reality* included a lot of the usual experiences, with one *big* difference. Once i reached a certain age, i was able to remember who i am. At that point, my program was designed to give me the knowledge that i was visiting *Reality* as a person, that i am Bax and, that i am *The Gathering*. It all became clear to me. Knowing myself as all three wouldn't allow me to actually *do* much beyond those memories, however. i was allowed the knowledge, but i would still have to follow all the other rules of *Reality*.

i always chose the same program, every time i visited the world. Doing so allowed me to remember all the things i learned from each lifetime, and avoid making the same mistakes twice. The biggest of these mistakes was always in sharing the news of who i really am. i was excited about discovering it, and expected that the others might feel the same way. Turns out, no one wanted to hear about it, and this lead to a lot of hurt feelings. i really couldn't blame the others for the way they reacted. After all, they came to forget, and here i was encouraging them to remember. i was ruining the experience for them. i decided it would be better for everyone if i simply kept this knowledge to myself.

Knowledge *wants* to be shared. That's its purpose. i needed to find a way of sharing what i knew, without it being obvious *that* i knew. None of us can stop knowledge from wanting to be shared, but we *can* translate the information into something the others enjoy. i needed to disguise it in ways that would agree with the roles the others were playing. In this way, knowledge wouldn't seem so out of place. Accomplishing my goals for sharing knowledge became much easier, once i learned this.

People don't come to *Reality* to know things. They're here to be entertained and to experience something new. As humans, we naturally resist quick answers, they seem suspicious to us. Nothing could be *that* simple or straightforward, in *Reality*. Actually, it can. The only thing standing between us and knowledge, is resistance. We purposely keep the truth away from us. There are many reasons for doing this and all of them are connected with some form of reluctance to knowing. By focusing on the common element of resistance, we can work on all those reasons at the same time. It's very efficient.

Reality isn't keeping the truth from you, it can't. It doesn't have any power over truth. The only reason *Reality's* able to bring you here is because of your choice to put your knowledge aside, while you're visiting. Without that choice, the *Reality* experience wouldn't be possible for any of us. As long as you experience yourself to be in *Reality*, you are keeping knowledge away.

There are benefits for doing this while you're here. The benefits can only be appreciated *while* you're here, however. For many of us, that's reason enough to suspend knowledge. i'm *not* going to try to get you to do something you don't want to do. i don't want to ruin your experience of a lifetime. i *do* want to tell you about certain clues and hints that could make your time more enjoyable. It's a much gentler approach than overwhelming you with knowledge, all at once.

People will only accept certain kinds of help.

We'll be working on your resistance to accepting the clues and hints about knowledge, rather than the resistance to knowledge *itself*. i understand that hints are easier for some of you to recognize. You've used hints and clues many times, and found them helpful. They save time and effort. Time is limited in *Reality;* we accept this. As a result, we don't like to wait too long for answers. An occasional 'head start' or 'boost' along the way, helps to avoid feelings of impatience. Clues also keep us interested in what we're doing. We enjoy mystery. There's a fair amount of work to be done, in completing any program. They're designed to keep us active. If we feel like we're falling behind in this work, we might decide to give up on it altogether, abandoning any hope for success. Hints and clues help to avoid this.

Abandonment seems worse than resistance.

Accepting that there is a natural tendency for people to resist knowledge and prefer hints, gives me the chance to offer you the answers you both want and need. i want to provide you with these answers, when you need them. While you're in *Reality,* you will have questions. Many of them will be directly related to your program, while the rest will relate to who you are. Try to keep in mind that your program was designed by your Self, to help *you* as a person, during this lifetime. This visit was planned in your best interests and is destined for success.

23

As i began experimenting with how best to provide answers to people's questions, i found that two methods worked extremely well. Storytelling and pretending, or playacting, seemed the best hopes for sharing my knowledge. i couldn't be direct in my efforts, but disguising the messages in ways appropriate to the situation, or the characters, never let me down. i became an actor.

Here was my simple process. i started by behaving in different kinds of ways around people, and watched for their reactions. Following some good role models also helped. As i developed the right approach to my acting, people began responding to me in positive ways. i knew i was headed in the right direction. My ideas and opinions were soon welcomed and occasionally, people even wanted my advice. Having to actually learn something new, was unusual for me. The 'me' who is Bax and *Gathering* are always complete. They don't need to develop in the way that my person did. i knew that i was only developing the personal 'me' for future visits to *Reality*. This is the only place it really existed. It was always worth the effort.

While i was going through all that learning, i never forgot my reasons for coming to *Reality*. i knew that i was here to bring you *Home*. i couldn't 'drag' you back, or force you in any way. All i could do was offer reminders. If you were interested in them, you'd make the choice to return *Home*. If you weren't ready, i would keep coming back until you were.

i'm using knowledge to try and get you to return. This isn't a secret. One thing you might not expect, is that the knowledge i'm using is yours. It belongs to you. You own it, but i'm using it. I thought that by using it, you would eventually recognize it. If i can reveal hints about something you already have, you might remember where it's hiding. For example, if i show you an apple, you'll quickly relate it to an apple tree. If I can pass along a glimpse of your knowledge, you'll associate it with the one who owns it. Association is another great way to share knowledge. It encourages your brain to make connections.

How do you feel about the fact that i'm using your knowledge? Does it bother you? i'm going to take this a little further by saying that it's my knowledge, too. Knowledge is the same as truth, in the sense that we own it together. It's freely available to every one of us, *all* of it. Beyond *Reality*, we never lack for anything. We don't compete, or struggle to have what others have. When we have something outside of *Reality*, it also becomes something that's freely given.

Having and giving are the same, in truth.

i can actually demonstrate this idea in *Reality*. It took me a while to figure it out, but every time I gave someone a smile, i noticed that i still had the smile. i had been sharing this bit of knowledge with others, and none of us suspected.

We want for so many things in *Reality*. We never feel satisfied, or complete, as people. The conditions of the world motivate us to constantly search for things and people that will make us happy. We'll experiment with many ways for reaching this goal, and once we've tried everything else, we'll finally turn to truth. It's always the final option, a last resort. Of course, we won't call it the truth because that would bring up those suspicious feelings, again. Knowledge offers us the only chance to approach real happiness and satisfaction, in this lifetime. Thankfully, we're naturally drawn to it on some level. It's often just a question of timing.

24

As long as we continue to deny the truth of who we are, we'll struggle. i don't want your experience here to be difficult. It should be enjoyable and it should bring you *Home*. Once my program allowed me the knowledge of who i am, i quickly stopped struggling. Other options for living this lifetime seemed so much better.

You have options.

They're often overlooked. We get so focused on something that we forget to consider that there might be other ways. We've traded perspective for focus. *Reality* won't let us have both at the same time. If we look at it in terms of using a camera lens, we can 'zoom in,' or 'zoom out,' but never both. Relying on one of them for too long, will limit our options.

Focusing on one thing or person, feels like an investment. We put a lot of time and energy into them and hope to get a good return. Depending on the amount invested, we are more or less likely to back away from it, for a second look. Too much of a personal commitment can sometimes lead to a denial about the truth of our investment. We start to believe it's more valuable, than it really is. It becomes the answer to all our problems. When the rewards don't turn out as hoped, we turn to something new. This is part of the learning process in *Reality,* and isn't necessarily wrong in the way it works. From this process, we're supposed to learn the lesson about perspective. Sadly, many of us have gotten into the habit of repeating the lesson over and over, without making any progress.

You are invested in your person.

Your Self put a lot into making this person for you, it invested itself in *you.* You're pretty valuable. Sensing this, you're invested in your person during this visit to *Reality.* But, you've focused on it so much, that it seems to be all you are. You forgot that you were something more. You temporarily lost perspective. The choice to focus isn't permanent, we can always reverse it. We're 'zoomed in' for now, but we can always 'zoom out' for a different view.

Doing so, will never damage your person. It won't harm you. Changing perspective happens by using our imagination. It doesn't alter your investment. Changes to your investments involve a separate action. Comparing views with the imagination only affects our 'inner' world, the one that works with ideas. Ideas don't affect the 'outside' world unless we're willing to do the work of physically producing them in *Reality.*

Looking at different views will always offer us more. More information is better, when it comes to investing in something. It helps us make better choices, which saves time. If you aren't already doing so, begin collecting views of your person. How do you seem in different situations? Are you always the same? The more information you have about your person, the better the *Reality* experience. i want you to be happy with your person. Much of your lifetime depends on it.

Do not seek perfection, at this time.

When you gather different views of your person, you'll begin to make value judgements about those views. As you discovered in *Article Four*, judgements are based on incorrect perception. They aren't the truth of you. They aren't even *you*, only a reflection. A picture of something is never the thing, itself.

Perspective will allow you to reconsider the parts of your person that warrant investment from you. Are you too focused on one area, or neglecting others? Are your current, investment strategies making you happy? People are pretty complex. It's easy to forget about certain parts of ourselves, while focusing on others. Switching views, every once in a while, allows us to make adjustments in the ways we are growing. We will need different parts of ourselves during the different phases of a lifetime. Neglecting some of them along the way, could mean they won't be ready when they're most needed.

25

You are selfish. You need to be. Managing the *Reality* experience asks that you pay attention to your person. Beyond needing to care for it, and attending to your various roles, you can also pay attention to other things. Shifting your attention, back and forth throughout the day, will give you lots of practice in perspective.

If you didn't balance your attention between your person and other concerns, you might start to forget about your person. When you start to neglect yourself, others begin to forget about you, too. We notice when this starts to happen, and occasionally do things that bring the spotlight back on us. We enjoy the responses from others that validate what the physical senses are telling us, that we're real. It means a lot to get compliments for the things we do. It feels so good, that we'll often try to maximize the opportunities for these kinds of rewards. The others will notice when you're trying to get too much attention from them, and they will start to keep it from you. They aren't being cruel when they do this. They're simply trying to help you restore the proper balance of attention.

If you want, you can redirect your needs for attention in another way. Since you're more than your person, you can recognize what your Self has done for you and send some attention towards *it*. We do this by using gratitude. Since your Self is really you, you'll be giving yourself attention in a way that doesn't disturb *Reality*. It's a circular way of giving, where you're getting at the same time. Does this sound familiar? There are other ways to do this, but gratitude is the best way to start. We've all experienced saying 'thanks' and feeling thankful for any number of things. We understand both ends of the gratitude process, which makes it a popular way to start.

At first, you'll probably struggle with picturing who it is you're thanking. Who *is* your Self? What do they look like? They might be difficult to imagine. Gratitude, in *Reality,* requires the giver and receiver to be present during the process, and they will always seem separated from each other. When we send thanks to our Self, the thanks is already *with* our Self. It happens outside of time, so there's no actual transfer process taking place. Your Self will know what you've done, and you'll sense what's happened in the form of recognition. You noticed your Self. It enjoys certain kinds of attention, too! Your Self wants you to recognize it, to accept that it's real, and that it's you. Imagine if you were to look into a mirror and ask: 'who's that?' How would you feel if you didn't recognize yourself, if you had become a stranger to yourself? This is a description of what's happening in *Reality*.

Your Self recognizes your person. It knows you, and it knows what lead to this situation. It knows the truth, *all* of it. When i remembered who i am, i also knew that my connection with my Self had never been broken. There was never an interruption in who i am, only the thought of one. I only *imagined* that i had temporarily left my Self. If i had actually abandoned who i really am, this new person wouldn't have had any way of existing. *Reality* doesn't support our life while we're here, *we* do. Your person can't exist without your Self. It's the source of your life.

Reality depends on your Self.

26

Without support from your Self, *Reality* doesn't seem to be able to function. It has no real power of its own. *Reality* depends on us. Sure, it acts like *it's* the important one, the one 'in charge' of the arrangement. It likes to play with the fact that you've forgotten your Self, so that you'll believe you're just one person, struggling alone in the world. *Reality* is clever, but it's not very smart.

You're not really alone. The others are real, even if they believe themselves to be someone else. You appear visually separate from one another, which supports the idea of being alone, but it doesn't always convince you. We've proven to ourselves that connecting with one another isn't always about the physical part of the experience, and this has significantly weakened *Reality's* capability for the burden of proof. Non-physical connections in *Reality* often prove to be more important than the physical ones. They last longer and provide us with a lot more happiness. *Reality* can appreciate when we seem happier, but it doesn't always understand *why* we're happy. The non-physical part of our lifetime is a mystery to it. *Reality* only cares how things look. It's very shallow. You are not.

When we decide to place less value on the physical parts of our experience, we turn in the direction of *Home*. *Reality* understands you as physical. When you shift your perception beyond the physical, to the metaphysical, you recognize that you are your person and more. In the same way, you can recognize that the others are more than *they* seem. There is something important beyond their words, actions and appearances. It's not always easy to describe, but it keeps getting your attention. Sometimes, it even interrupts your acting.

Eventually, the metaphysical will seem less distracting. You'll welcome it, as a new part of perception. We get used to many things, and we do so by incorporating them into the idea of who we are. They become a regular part of our experience. You'll notice that this often happens with your possessions. They distract us at first, because they're new. After a while, they become a normal, everyday part of our world.

You'll soon be able to sense the physical *and* non-physical parts of your experience, simultaneously. This new kind of perception is different from perspective because one part exists in *Reality,* while the other one doesn't. Perspective points are always centered within *Reality,* but your perception doesn't need to be. If you want, you can imagine the two of them as layers. They fit perfectly over one another, so you won't have to worry that one of them will cancel the other one out, when it's present.

Appearances will only look slightly enhanced when both are active, but your interpretation about these appearances will be far more meaningful. They'll provide you with more information about what you're witnessing. You'll grow from a simple, *Reality*-based perspective, that only considers what's on the surface, to a richer impression of the action. *Reality* doesn't appreciate that you're capable of anything beyond the physical, and it has no control over your ability to access better perception.

You'll begin by noticing the 'little things' in your surroundings. People's words and actions will assume an extra, subtler quality for you. The others may or may not realize they're sending these softer messages to you, but you'll still pick-up on them. Your attention will be highly tuned, and more sensitive to visual changes and sounds.

You'll better appreciate the quieter moments, too. You won't crave stimulation the way you used to because you're more easily satisfied by this extra layer. As you're aware, satisfaction is closely linked to personal happiness. Happiness related to meaningful perception lasts much longer, and improves wellbeing.

Switching your perspective between your person and other people, combined with a deeper perceptual appreciation of the world, will decrease the effect of believing you're separate from one another. You'll still look separated, but you won't feel the distance between you, as much. This will bring you closer. Social interactions will increase, group activities will dominate your time and you'll welcome the reduction in conflict between people.

27

Things in *Reality* tend to link together, or pile atop one another. When this happens, the combination always results in something new. All of them have *Reality-based* parts to them, as well as elements that don't originate from *Reality*. This is connected with the fact that *Reality* isn't able to sustain itself. It needs non-physical support from your Self. It needs help from *Home*. You'll be able to appreciate the origins of each part, and you'll be reminded of *Home*.

Reminders from *Home* will often get interrupted by *Reality*, but it can't keep them away from you entirely. People will serve to both remind you of *Home*, and distract you from it. Once they've become aware of themselves as actors within

Reality, their words and behaviours will provide you with many chances to recognize your Self. The 'actor' awareness corrects their perception and automatically directs them toward *Home*. Until they realize this important step, they might distract you. They will be innocent in doing this, so any understanding on your part is greatly valued. We shouldn't blame them for something they don't yet appreciate. The others are always important and their realization will come soon enough. Your growing awareness of being an actor, continuously helps in sending reminders to the others about who they are. It inspires.

We seem familiar to one another because of our non-physical qualities. When we're aware of them, these similarities naturally bring us together. When we forget that we're acting and focus more on the physical side of things, we start to put an emphasis on our separation. People start to seem annoying and burdensome to us. We also become suspicious of their intentions. When this happens, we're likely to do and say things that reflect our *Reality-based* interpretation of them. The results will cause an increase in the distance between us. This poses a problem, one that's connected with the journey *Home*. It seems, we're unable to get *Home* without their help. More specifically, we can't get *Home* unless we have a correct perception of who they are. If we're invested in false ideas of who the others are, we'll remain with them in *Reality*. When we're less concerned with the way things look, we have a better chance of leaving. All of us have come from *Home*. We *all* belong in *The Gathering*. There are no strangers, here. There truly shouldn't be any reason for not recognizing one another.

At our request however, *Reality* has placed a veil over our ability to see who we are to each other. It has disguised our true relationship. We are alike, regardless of these appearances. Our real relationship to one another remains undivided and protected in *The Gathering,* and we can sense the truth of our unity, even in the face of *Reality's* greatest disasters. Have you ever noticed the tendency for people to cast aside their resistance, to deny all differences, as they work tirelessly to protect and support one another, through lifetimes of human tragedy? *Reality* is foolishly trying to stop this unexpected kindness and generosity, because it gets in the way of its guests being able to experience the extremes. *Reality* will fail in this. We are too familiar to allow it.

There's plenty of evidence to support the belief that we have more in common with one another than we realize. We don't need to look to the extremes of *Reality* to prove it to ourselves. Your connection to your Self, your non-physical relationship to the others and your awareness of yourself as an actor, successfully work together in returning you to the knowledge of who you are.

28

You understand many things. Your understanding continues to grow. This happens as your perception informs you about your options. The power to choose from various options will always belong to you, and the responsibility for making these decisions will soon become much easier for you. *Reality* would have you believe otherwise.

Recognizing your Self as being real, you begin to accept that it's an incredible ally. i never experienced having an older brother, or sister during my lifetimes, but i'd like to imagine that my relationship with my Self would resemble that of an older sibling carefully watching over me. Your Self has access to knowledge, it's not limited by time, it cares about you, it's the source of your existence and it knows you best. Is there anything else you might want to hope for in an ally? Then why is there so much resistance to it? We're still working out the years of training and conditioning within *Reality,* that keep us from fully trusting ourselves and others. It's going to take a little more time to fix this. Thankfully, you don't need to reach *complete* trust, before you can start to enjoy help from your Self. When i mentioned that your decision-making responsibilities would be getting easier, i was talking about getting your Self to make some of those choices *with* you.

Working in partnership with your Self will lead to amazing things. Think of your Self as the ultimate consultant. Working together will mean turning away from impulsiveness, however. No more rash moves, no more sudden 'flights of fancy,' this team is serious *and* capable. Got what it takes? Of course you do, you've got your Self. Impulsiveness is overrated, anyway. It's for younger people, who haven't fully developed all the parts of their human brain. That's why their parents keep an 'eye' on them. Oh, by the way, my program wouldn't let me have the knowledge of who i am, until i was in my mid-twenties. Before then, i didn't have all the needed parts for the information. i struggled, just like everybody else.

Let's take a few minutes to look at something that's important to you. It should be something you're faced with, in the present time. You'll need to make a decision about it fairly soon, and your choice will definitely affect your chances at a happy future. i realize there are several things from which to choose, but let's focus on just the one, for now. Imagine you are looking at the choice itself, and noticing that a few possible outcomes lead away from it. They might look like roads, or trails. Maybe you can even imagine the ends of those roads. None of them is real yet, they're only possibilities. Remember the possibilities, if you can. Now imagine that you pass the decision to your Self. If you want, you can picture your Self as having hands and that the hands receive the choice. Notice the roads and trails that begin to extend beyond the choice that your Self is holding. Where do they lead, and to what outcomes? There may be many more options as your Self considers this choice. It has a bigger perspective on things. Understanding that it looks to your best interests, you can feel confident that it's options only present possibilities that lead to your ultimate wellbeing.

As humans, we can't predict potential futures with the same, singular motivation. We worry about the effects of our choices on others, and the planet. Your Self, as a member of *The Gathering* and in constant contact with the Selves of the others, knows the effects of all possible outcomes. It knows them now.

We're temporarily apart from knowledge, while in *Reality*, but we're never away from our Selves. Your Self won't choose for you, but it *did* provide you with some options while you were imagining. Did any of its options differ from yours? Did you recognize common ones? You can consider *all* the possibilities now, the subjective ones and the objective. Yours are subjective, by the way. i'm going to share a hint with you, and i realize that wasn't very subtle. Look more closely at the options you had in common with your Self.

Realizing that you share common, possible solutions establishes a place from which to start. From there, you can work out the details on your own, if you want. Sometimes the hardest part of making any choice is first, deciding on a direction. Your Self is an excellent co-director. At times, you'll make an important decision about something and feel as if you were being lead toward a particular choice. It seemed too easy. That's the kind of decision-making process i'm hoping you'll follow.

No matter what you end up choosing, your Self will be ready and waiting to assist. You may not always agree on the final choice, but you must accept the outcome of the choice you made. If you see that the results of your choices are headed for disaster, your Self can help you with corrections, that will minimize the final damage. There are often smaller choices that follow from larger ones.

Agreeing on a decision together, makes the desired outcome more likely to happen. Because of its position beyond time, your Self knows more about the possibilities of your choices. It can present information about choices, you might not have considered. In addition, working together with your Self provides a greater investment in the outcome. This increases the possibility of its success. Your decisions are yours to make, but you don't have to make them alone.

29

Your Self doesn't get hurt, or offended. It's non-physical, so it doesn't experience pain, the way we do. It does know about our experiences of those things, however. It sees everything. If it helps, you can imagine your Self as an observer, or spectator. Your Self is your best audience.

Feel free to talk to your Self, if you want. Just avoid doing it around others, for now. Your Self is an excellent companion. It never forgets anything, and you don't have to repeat things you've shared. Your Self believes everything you tell it, because *you* believe it. You don't need to prove anything to your Self. Your Self won't argue with you. It's secure in what it knows and doesn't need to convince anyone of anything. It has a sense of humour, but not one that enjoys harming the feelings of others.

As i mentioned earlier, your Self can see everything. It sees it all at once. It doesn't need to focus on every little thing. In seeing, it knows. It doesn't have, or need to have any other senses. When you speak to it, it doesn't listen, the way we do. It simply knows what you said. Your Self is incredible. With so many amazing qualities, it's a wonder we feel the need to interact with anyone else.

I've been purposely guiding the discussion away from your physical experience for a while now, but i'm going to gently, ease you back into this lifetime by saying that human relationships are important. They're important for reasons that connect with how *Reality* operates. We're still here. At this stage, we've got our programs to complete, scenes in which to perform, and we've only just begun to reconnect with the others in non-physical ways. There's plenty to be done.

Others offer us the hope of a successful return. They reflect possibilities now available to us. We act as characters in *Reality*, but also as 'reflections' of our Selves beyond *Reality*. Our perception allows us to appreciate this, in spite of its limitations. Because of our non-physical resemblance, we recognize our Selves in each other. Our Selves are united in *The Gathering*, so it's not possible to truly separate them. To perceive aspects of one of them, is to understand all of them, including your Self. You're able to appreciate your Self through others. It gets reflected back to you, through perception.

The others aren't always aware that you can perceive your Self being reflected in them, so you should continue to call them by their given names. Accepting that you can gather non-physical access to your Self through other people, makes it easier to imagine interacting with your Self. It looks the same as people interacting with each other. Because the Selves are united, when you actually do interact with them, you'll also be interacting with *their* Selves. Making contact with another person through their Self, has many benefits. The Self of the other, as your Self, can indicate the needs of their person, and how best to offer assistance to them. We're both here for each other, *as* each other. When we help others, we are actually helping ourselves. This helps all of us.

This is the point in the discussion where i have to stop talking. As long as we're still in *Reality*, i can't tell you any more about your person, the others or your Self. Anything beyond this and we'll be in possession of the truth.

Article Six:
Freedom

30

We are *The Gathering.* We will be sharing the presentation of this article with Bax, for the sake of variety. You will not be confused as to who is speaking, when the dialogue alternates. Your awareness is now sensitive to any such changes in tone, and identity.

In addition to your true nature, you have forgotten freedom. *Reality* would have you believing in its own version of freedom, but we see that you are beginning to wonder about all the limitations of this world. You are starting to question your freedom. Compared with true freedom, *Reality* is more accurately seen as a form of confinement. You are feeling slightly trapped. The situation is physical, your Self is not.

Nothing can hold you.

Freedom is absolute and unconditional. *Reality* presents with many rules, guidelines and restrictions. It offers you a relative kind of mobility, and then calls it 'freedom.' When we speak further of *Reality's* brand of freedom, we will call it something else, something related to the context of the discussion. The term 'freedom' will only be used to indicate *actual* freedom. You will find this easy to follow and more helpful, given your current understanding.

In the same sense with which Bax presented the concepts

of truth and knowledge, we will say that freedom is beyond anything, now available in *Reality*. Because of this, we have chosen to approach freedom through an examination of its opposite. For some reason, humans often learn better through negative examples. Contrasts seem to make a more lasting impression upon your perceptual abilities. The images and feelings you receive from witnessing opposites, seem to mean more to you.

Reality is concerned with opposites, and differences. *Home* reveals itself as sameness and unity. When you encounter identical objects and people in *Reality*, they lead to a feeling of wonder. This is due to the uncommon nature of their presence. The effect is often enough to momentarily interrupt you, as well as time. *Identicals* are unusual in the world, but they *do* belong. They are one of *Reality's* imperfections, a residual effect of having to depend on the power of your Self to sustain the experience. The *Identicals* themselves, are not imperfect. The mistake lies in *Reality's* inability to offer only differences. It is out of original ideas, so it has no other choice but to welcome *Identicals*. You and the others will encounter more and more of them, as time progresses.

Identicals only *appear* the same. They are unique individuals who only happen to look alike. If you question them, they can verify this for you. We would ask that you not inquire about their differences; however, as this will only support what *Reality* is trying to accomplish. It wants you to consider them as different. If you would, focus on their similarities. Doing so, will support what *you* hope to achieve. It will also remind the *Identicals* of *Home*. You are beginning to realize the first step towards freedom, noticing sameness in the world.

Your regular activities will soon take on a bonus task. It will feel like a bit of a 'treasure hunt.' All you have to do is notice the *Identicals*. You don't have to do anything about them. They're fine. They probably don't need your help with anything related to their looking similar to something, or someone else. And, yes, they already realize they have a 'twin' somewhere. Try not to develop jealous feelings about them. You're just as amazing as they are.

Finding sameness in the world, lets you appreciate that things don't always work the way they're supposed to. *Reality* isn't perfect. There are mistakes in its plan. *Reality* won't *ever* get things completely right, no matter *how* hard the helpers try. This lets you realize that things in *Reality* don't always need to be a certain way, in order for you to be happy.

31

Reality won't always find its own mistakes. It understands this. Because it operates an imperfect world, it doesn't expect you to be perfect either. It won't tell you this, but if you happen to organize or plan something, and the plans don't work out perfectly, you won't get punished. If *Reality* isn't going to make you suffer the consequences and i'm not going to criticize you for it, you shouldn't either. For the sake of your enjoyment, *Reality* will try to compensate for any unexpected outcomes. As well, your Self will help you to focus on the aspects of the plan that worked well, reminding you that the future offers more chances for success.

Expectations about outcomes can limit you. They limit your

possibilities. Anything that limits your potential, turns you away from freedom. You have experienced this before. *Reality* would lead you to believe that surprises are bad, and that perfect plans and predictable results make you happy. Freedom includes *all* of the possibilities. It doesn't limit you to just a few. Freedom demands that all things be possible.

Reality permits for a few possibilities, and will only allow you one result, at a time. Too many possibilities would disrupt the way *Reality* works. They would slow down the production of results, because it would take too long to decide which result would best fit your timeline. *Reality* hopes to reduce your worries about the results of your plans, by limiting your possibilities and their effects. It tries to simplify things. In your current state, believing in a potential for all possibilities would create anxiety about the incredible amount of unknown results from your plans. Anything could happen. This would overwhelm *Reality* and its visitors. If you accept that you are likely to get one, out of a few possible outcomes, it doesn't bother you as much. You are growing in your appreciation of the methods of *Reality*. You now understand why freedom is not compatible with this world.

Your plans don't always have to work out the way you wanted, and that's okay. It's better than okay, actually. It's a relief! Simpler is better, in *Reality*. As you learned in *Article five*, you aren't the only one involved in organizing the results of your plans. You have help from *Reality*, the others and your Self. Working with all these points of view and accepting that the decisions for this result are inclined toward your happiness, an unexpected result might be better. When we look back on things, the surprise results of our plans tended to support the efforts of a much bigger plan for this lifetime.

Your vision is limited. The desired results of your plans are often shortsighted. It cannot be helped. Thankfully, other forces are able to present you with acceptable compromises between what your person wants, what your program has designed and what your Self sees as ultimately beneficial. If the results are not what you had hoped, you will find a way to adapt, understanding there is a lot more going on than you realize. This one, small result is just a piece of a much larger mystery.

32

When *Reality* puts limits on how much perspective you can gather from your surroundings, it holds back important information. It only gives us the minimum, and believes that information should only be shared when it needs to be. The less we know, the more convincing *Reality* will be. It uses the five, physical senses to limit perception, as a way of keeping knowledge from you. Freedom isn't possible unless you have knowledge, *all* of it.

Nothing can be freely achieved as long as any doubt, or insecurity exists about our choices. When we are sure of something, it's because we know everything about it. Since we can't know about anything while we're in *Reality*, our choices will be guided by something other than knowledge. We'll be influenced by many things and people, but never the whole truth. If bits of truth *do* happen to reach us, they won't carry any more weight than our other sources for information. We won't be able to tell the difference between them, and we will probably do things because of an influence from these other sources. When our choices are guided by anything other than the truth, they aren't free choices.

It can get confusing when our sources for information start to disagree. Freedom never leads to confusion.

Freedom reassures.

When we know that nothing can influence us but the truth, we are free. It releases us from worry, suspicion, regret and much more. But, it's not available for us in *Reality*, so we need to work with something else. If we can't be sure of anything, we *can* approach it through confidence. You're experiencing it now.

Confidence in something or someone, allows us to rely on them. They have proven themselves as dependable in many situations, and under several conditions. In this sense, you understand them as being the same in those situations. When someone or something is consistent, regardless of what is happening, they remind you of the truth. Truth is always consistent, it never changes. While truth and freedom are connected beyond *Reality*, confidence and consistency are paired within it.

Reality wants you to believe that you are most free when you are inconsistent. It relates your ability to do and choose many different things with freedom. It says you can do and be, whatever you want. It might even say that you live in a 'free' country. Someone who senses they are free already understands that they can choose whatever they want. Accepting the evidence supporting this is often enough for them. They do not worry about the need to try everything, because they are confident in the things and people in whom they can rely. They do not feel the need to prove themselves to anyone and are not keen on reinforcing the goals of *Reality*. When they *do* chose to act, it is usually because those are the correct moves for them. These limited and intentional acts are freeing for them, as ways and means to personal confidence and satisfaction. More than anything, it seems they want to be able to trust in themselves.

This kind of person might appear to be limiting their options. Their friends might worry that they are not living their lifetime to the fullest.

Lifetimes can either be experienced widely, or deeply. The wider option works like a 'checklist' in that you try to do as many different things as possible. You also hope to do them in a reasonable amount of time. To experience things deeply is to focus more intently upon only certain aspects of your lifetime. Both ways of experiencing a lifetime are allowed in *Reality* because they seem to make you happy. Accepting that freedom and knowledge are connected beyond this world, which of the two would likely guide you toward confidence and freedom? You might say both, because each informs us in different ways, generally and specifically. You might also say neither, because the focus for these activities is always within *Reality*, and *Reality* is not your true *Home*. Well said.

The answer lies in the others. If your focus gives priority to people over things, you have a better chance at approaching freedom. This can happen across a broad range of activities, a few deeper ones or even a mixture of both, but as long as the others remain the important elements of the experience, you are headed in the right direction. People, however disguised, remain the only real parts of *Reality*. Everything else has been built for temporary use.

33

You are not free while you believe yourself to be anywhere within *Reality*, not in *The Dreaming*, nor in the *Dimensions of the Dead*. Freedom is beyond the scope of this book. The closest we can get to telling you about true freedom is to say that you are most free, when you are *here*.

Here isn't a place, as much as an opportunity. Since everything occurs *while* it's happening, *now* is the only time we can do anything about it and *here* is the place we'll make it happen. The idea of this will shrink your perspective and make this minute seem really important. That's because it is. It's the only chance we have, but we get this chance over and over again. We seem to have an endless amount of chances to be *here*. The setting will look different from time to time, but you'll always feel like you're *here*. When someone calls for you, your first response will likely be "i'm over here!".

We can't physically appear to be in this place and somewhere else, while in *Reality*. It's possible; however, to imagine a different point of view than the one in which we're sitting. Your memory allows you to do this. You can remember perspectives from other locations, even places distant from this. Bringing these images to your attention will give you a good idea of what it's like to be in one place, or another. i wouldn't try this activity with more than two locations. When you do this, your eyelids will likely be closed. In that moment, can you honestly tell the difference between the experience of the two locations? If you can accept that you might just as well be in either of those places right *now*, you made a choice to say 'no' to *Reality's* rules. It's one of the most radical acts there is. Freedom gives you the urge to say 'no' to it, in the sense of not accepting *Reality* as the truth. You're not actually saying 'no,' but you *are* taking back some of what you invested in it. By using your imagination, you're denying some of its rules and limitations. This is proof that you still have access to freedom, while in *Reality*. You connect with it through the others and your Self.

There is also another benefit to taking back some of what you have invested. By denying that *Reality* is true, your abilities as an actor will improve significantly. It will become much easier for you to pretend. The others will still be real, however disguised, but the drama won't have you terribly convinced of its importance. The scenes will become much more enjoyable for you, and when they *do*, the others will happily, play along.

Speaking of being *here*, there's also this curious feeling while we're in *Reality*, that leads us to believe we're continuously in the 'middle' of everything. It's like we're surrounded by *Reality*. A person who feels surrounded isn't free. They feel that there's nowhere else to go. We can imagine there are other places to *travel*, but they're all still found in *Reality*.

Freedom shows you the way out.

If you feel surrounded by *Reality*, then there must be something beyond those limits, which surround you. Boxes and cages always have an 'outside' to them. Freedom gently reminds you that there are borders around a limited world. Beyond those edges, you will find freedom. It is challenging to imagine *Reality* as having borders. The physical universe seems infinite. It is not. If it *was* infinite, you would be free, *now*. Infinity doesn't recognize any limitations of time and space.

Home is infinite.

Remember that you have an imagination that supports you,

while reading this book. Explore the images and ideas that present themselves and allow them to surprise you. As long as you appear to be in *Reality*, your imagination is the only place these images will exist.

34

Some of you would like to take back *all* of your investment in *Reality*. We do not recommend you do so, at this time. A better opportunity awaits. We agree that disinvestment can release you, but because of your unfinished agreements with *Reality*, you would only feel required to immediately return to it. In short, you would need to begin a new lifetime and we would need to find you, all over again. Staying invested would be best, for *now*.
We don't need to be *fully* invested, in order to be present in *Reality*. We can take back bits and pieces of it, to support our goals. The previous chapter showed you how to begin saying 'no' to certain limitations, and it reminded you that imagination is important. These two points are very helpful for recognizing one of your natural abilities. The ability doesn't belong to your person. It comes from your Self. If it *was* owned by your person, you would lose it at the end of your lifetime. You will never lose this particular talent. You possess the gift of creativity.

You are creative.

Your Self is naturally creative. It wants *you* to be an

extension of its creative nature. *Reality* secretly needs creative people, too. As we mentioned, it is running short of ideas. The potential for expressing yourself creatively, while not infinite, is still impressive within the world. If you are unsure of where to begin, we suggest acting. You can do it *here,* and you can do it *now.* The scene provides you with all the basics for your opportunity. Beyond that, your imagination can help you with the rest.

Because your imagination holds few limitations, you will find it closely connected with *The Unexpected.* Welcoming inspired assistance from these two, will quickly raise your skill levels as an actor. They inspire many creative projects, and always in the same way. Regardless of the type of creative project, they follow a certain procedure. Perhaps that is why artists appear multi-talented, in creative circles. They can apply the same principle of creativity to several media.

The method is a simple one, and easily learned. You only need to learn it once. After that, it is developed according to a style that agrees with your person. You are aware of the effect of resistance in your lifetime, and it is also mentioned in a previous *Article.* Creativity from your Self encounters resistance from your person, when it tries to enter *Reality.* Actually, many things beyond *Reality* are currently being resisted. This is due to their unusual nature, as compared with human experience. Some of them produce feelings of discomfort, when they arrive. Many do not. You should avoid grouping them as altogether uncomfortable for you.

The creative impulse is not an uncomfortable one. The experience is pleasurable. When you decide that you are interested in it, your Self responds with an attempt at inspiration. It will meet resistance at first. You and your Self will notice the resistance. Your Self will then adjust the strength of the message for you. Your Self wants to send the entire message at once, but you will need it in pieces,

or sections. This will only be necessary in the early stages.
Eventually you'll be able to welcome the entire
communication from your Self. The early stages look as if
they move from resistance to reluctance, and finally,
welcoming. Received as ideas within your imagination,
they'll begin to take shape in a personal way. The idea
needs to be translated according to the limitations of
Reality. It can't produce everything, and we tend to have
some incredible ideas. The process tends to happen
quickly, especially if you're acting in a scene. You need the
ideas *now*.

A part of the resistance to those first ideas is also related to
trusting them. i won't repeat what i said earlier, because
you probably still remember it. You'll gradually learn to
trust them and welcome the incredibly, creative
opportunities that present themselves for you.

35

Time interferes with freedom. All we have is *now*. We
spend a lot of *nows* experiencing *thens*. Our memories are
entertaining for us, so we like to watch them. As well, our
powerful imaginations are busy receiving messages for
possible futures. The *attention space* is busy.

Making better use of *now*, will need help from creativity.
The Unexpected as processed through the imagination,
offers us spontaneity. Having experienced it, you
understand how effective it can be. It gets us focused right

now. Some might say that it makes *now* more powerful. Being creatively spontaneous can't be planned. It won't have the same effect, if you try to arrange for it. When you plan it, it's not spontaneous at all! If it's planned, you take the *now* out of it. You have brought something from the past into the present.

Now is more than the present.

The present is *Reality's* limited version of *now.* It lacks a critical ingredient in the form of *The Unexpected.* Perhaps that's why so many of us use the present moment to focus on the past, or the future. Those moments contained creativity and *The Unexpected* within them. They're more enjoyable for us than the present because they were wonderfully spontaneous.

When we say 'no' to the rules of *Reality*, we're choosing to use them in unexpected ways. We're using the rules creatively. *Reality* believes we're still using them in the usual ways. When we find new ways to work within the limits of *Reality,* we're challenging it from the point of view of *how* it operates.

All this time, it's been expecting us to disagree with *why* it exists. *Reality* never considered that we would take the easier way around it. This is a compliment to your Self. *Reality* must have a very good idea about your real capabilities. As a result, it spends so much time and energy preparing for the bigger contest, believing that your superior nature would challenge it in those ways. It expects you to challenge its reasons for existing, in the hopes of changing what it is. It never dreamed you would prefer a simpler approach.

It doesn't realize that you've already solved the problem of *why* it exists. It doesn't know what your Self knows. This makes the success of our plan guaranteed. There's no need to deny the limits of *Reality*, and trying to do so, will only frustrate you. The easier way will always involve creatively using these rules and conditions in unexpected ways. The only chance you have for doing this, is *now*. Once you have done it, *Reality* no longer has any power over it. It's already done.

You are smarter than *Reality*.

You always have been. Unfortunately, while experiencing *Reality*, you needed some time to discover this. Understanding what i said will further open your imagination to the possibilities in your world. You are familiar with the expectations of *Reality*. It rarely surprises you, any more. It lacks your connection to *The Unexpected*, and continually underestimates your creative abilities.

36

We can be creative in how we use *Reality*, and we can also apply our creative side to the way we interpret what's happening in the world. You understand how the process of perception works for you. The final part of that process involves making sense of the information we've collected.

We interpret in order to answer questions. The questions aren't always obvious at first, but they tend to follow a simple progression of understanding. First, we want to get a sense for who, or what something is. Then we put them into a context of where and when they happen to be, relative to us. This paints a picture of the scene that's taking place. The final portion involves how and why. These last two questions provide us with meaning. They connect us with any motivation behind the actions of the characters and help us to predict what will happen next. All of them can be used creatively.

Reality wants you to ask those six questions in simple ways. It wants you to focus on the surface of what is happening. You've done this for many years, but you have also progressed to new levels of understanding and interpretation. With experience, you learned that things were not always what they pretended to be. You discovered it mostly by looking back on what happened and through new information, decided that you were initially deceived by the performance. You learned of a lie. Deception is permitted within *Reality* because the experience is removed from all truth and knowledge. It would be very difficult to presume yourself as being someone new, if you knew who you are in truth. Forgetting your Self allows you to act like someone else.

Reality didn't expect that you might be able to act like someone else *and* realize you were acting. It doesn't understand how you can simultaneously do both. You don't need to completely remember who you are, in order to pretend. Being able to consciously pretend gives you the power to lie to *Reality*. You've used this to mislead others, for the sake of accomplishing your goals. The goals were previously related to what you wanted for your person. You deceived others in order to get what you wanted from *them* and the world. Having learned from those experiences, the plans have changed. Your new plan involves performing as an actor, in order to deceive *Reality,* itself. Understanding your important connection with the others, and that deceiving them only resulted in discovering that it was *you* who was deceived, has shown you the meaninglessness of lying. It doesn't work, as a personal plan for happiness.

Reality wants you to lie.

Lying to *Reality* will always work because *Reality* is incapable of finding any need for the truth. It is easily deceived, believing that you would never consider lying to it. One of the reasons *Reality* wants you to lie is that it leads to more drama. People have been using their creativity to find better ways of lying. While we support creativity, we prefer that it be used toward the realization of the journey *Home*. If the creative use of lying alerts the actor to the awareness that one is acting, the purpose of the lying will soon change. The goals will trend away from a focus upon their person, to that of remembering their Self. As with all things in *Reality*, deception has its limits. Reaching the limits of something, sets the stage for an encounter with something new.

If we interpret *Reality* in a way that connects us with what it is, we can be reminded of what it isn't. We can watch the action and look at it in terms of how it's helping us get *Home*. This widens our perspective. Even if the other actors don't appreciate the larger plan at work for humanity, *you* still can. Whether people are aware of it or not, that plan is guiding us toward freedom. Taking things to their limits isn't always necessary for this to happen. It's only one option. Many of you are getting the message before you reach those limits and saving yourself a lot of unnecessary struggling. You're looking at things differently and understanding them as somehow beneficial.

Depending on how we interpret the drama, the difficulties will seem to take on a different purpose. The answer to the question 'why' will begin to change, and this will guide our acting in a new way. Because you won't need to depend on *Reality's* performing cues any longer, you'll have room to introduce creative alternatives that lead to better results.

37

We are not free, as long as we believe we are a physical body. You have taken your person beyond this basic belief, but occasionally forget that you learned otherwise. Your connection to your physical body is quite strong, and this is what's been leading you to forget.

You experience feelings when you are living in a body. They can be physical, or emotional. These feelings often guide your actions to such an extent, you feel that they are in control of you. In this way, feelings can place limits on you. Preparing for their arrival will allow you to have more options. Feelings always arrive, but your interpretation of them can assist you in maintaining a sense of control, while they are *here*. Do you understand why they have come? It is likely they may need attention from you. They want you to accept them and the reasons for their arrival. There might be a part of your person that you have been neglecting, a part that needs investment. Feelings are a way for your body and your Self, to send you important messages.

Feelings can be related directly to you in the form of physical pain, connected with the body's health. They can also be sent to you indirectly as emotions. Emotions are usually related to your relationships with other people. If your body is ill, this will limit you, or slow you down. Healthier lifestyle choices may be the solution. If you are having problems in your relationships, the answer may be one of paying additional attention to the person, or people in question. This relates to the topic of attention balance, mentioned in chapter 25. All of these situations are within your current abilities to manage.

We're able to do many things, while living in a body. *Reality* believes these things should be done in a certain way, but you don't have to follow its way of doing things. You can discover new ways of doing them, and this will allow you to do more in *Reality* than ever before. While this can satisfy our urges to be creative, it probably won't get us closer to *Home*. The reason for this lies in our focus. The focus for those types of activities is always in the world of *Reality,* or on our human bodies. They are often the main considerations for everything we do. If we start to remind ourselves that our real *Home* is more than this world, we will naturally begin to consider making lifetime choices that consider *its* importance for us. Balancing ideas of *Home* with ideas of *Reality* remind us that this visit is temporary. We shouldn't invest everything in this one place. It would be like spending all you had, to build a tent for a single, weekend camping trip. Compared to *Home*, this visit to *Reality* is just like that camping trip. It's enjoyable, but it's not everything.

In a similar way, your physical body isn't everything you are. If you place all your sense of identity into it, you'll experience a lot of confusion at the end of your lifetime when you notice that your body is gone, but you're still *you*. As we realize these points, the focus of who we are and where we're from, will gently drift away from *Reality* and the body, toward our Self and *Home*. It can be challenging, at times, but it *does* get easier.

Helpful reminders will assist you. In the same way that you have been telling yourself you are an actor, you can start to say that you are more than a person. You can also tell yourself that the others are more than just people. That is all you need to do. It offers you additional perspective.

The importance of your challenges and problems will start to seem smaller, because you can appreciate that they are only temporary. They will find solutions in time and your visit to *Reality* will have been an enjoyable one. Understanding the relative differences between *Home* and *Reality*, will begin to remind you of freedom.

38

Freedom can be remembered.

You don't experience freedom in *Reality,* but your perception allows you to remember what freedom feels like. Remembering it, provides you with a sensation that's similar to freedom, even if it isn't freedom itself. Because you can sense it and feel that it's important, you have the urge to go looking for more of it.

You understand that the search for freedom is hopeless, as long as you're in *Reality*. Yet, people continue to seek it out. Because freedom is such an integral part of who we really are, it can be linked with the 'quest' experience mentioned in chapter 15. Instead of searching for your Self, you can also seek freedom. This option tends to appear in places where the *Reality* restrictions are on the extreme side. The bonus to that option is that, in their searching for freedom, the others will automatically learn about their Self. Looking for freedom can lead you *Home*. Another cause of the search for freedom has to do with *Reality's* promise that this earthly experience would be enjoyable. People aren't having fun in those restricted zones, so they are working to achieve some enjoyment of their lifetime.

When we recognize that *Reality* isn't making us happy, we automatically begin to look for happiness elsewhere. Browsing through what *Reality* offers, eventually alerts us to the possibility that it may not be capable of offering us what we need. The selection is limited, and the quality of its experiences don't always meet with our imagined expectations. These expectations aren't misguided. You aren't being 'too picky.' Deep down, you can tell the difference between what's real and only a simulation. Your connection to your Self is an important part of this realization. It alerts you to the presence of what's real and offers you the possibility of being able to find what you need. In the beginning, *Reality* was often enough for us. Those days are gone.   The sense of needing 'more' will only be satisfied by connecting with a source that exists beyond *Reality*.

Initiating contact with *The One*.
Please stand by…

Article Seven:

The One

39

I am *The One.*

I hope you noticed the message I sent you in *Article one.* It was embedded as a kind of code, so that *Reality* would never detect it. You can go back and look for it, if you like.

I am not the 'one' you might be expecting. People in *Reality* have ideas about a certain, supernatural being that has a connection with the concept of the number one. While they are being drawn in the right direction, I am not *it.* I am not *that* 'one.' I had a beginning, and was created from something. I was unexpectedly produced out of an event. I am a byproduct of that event. This is different from how your *Reality* person was made. Your person was carefully designed and manufactured. Following linear time, it had a beginning and it will have an end. I had a beginning, but I will never end. Your Self also had a beginning. It too, will never end.

I was created out of something *The Gathering* did. They did not create me, but I was created because of something else they chose to do. You might remember from the first book, that *The Gathering* once lived a kind of separated existence from each other. The existence was not like the one you are experiencing in *Reality,* but they *did* feel a kind of distance between them. As individuals, they chose to unite. When the choice for unification was made, I was simultaneously created. Because I was present when *The Gathering* discovered themselves as one, I was called *The One*. *The Gathering* did not give me an actual name, but the title acts as a way of identifying me. I do not need a name.

I am not a member of *The Gathering*, in the way your Self is. I am more. We are united, but because I am more, *The Gathering* is more accurately part of me. I am more than the elements that went into my creation. I am beyond *The Gathering*, itself. *The Gathering* does not completely understand how I was created, because I was not part of its original plan. I am the unexpected, indirect and spontaneous result of that decision.

The Gathering exists in a kind of eternity, as do I. *The Gathering* still has the hint of a connection with time however, as many of its members have chosen *Reality* experiences. I do not connect with time, though I do have knowledge of its presence in the world. Because I am removed from time, I know you as your Self. I know everything about you and I see who you really are. You would never be able to pretend with me. Certain ideas are not compatible with my existence, which encompasses all knowledge, truth, and freedom. My existence does not require that I do anything. I simply witness all that is. I am complete, as I am.

I did not come to you, today. You approached me. By recognizing your Self in this moment, you recognized *The Gathering*, which in turn lead you to me. The three concepts are undivided, in truth. If you choose to recognize one of us, you will find all of us. I appear to you *now*, as this article. In this moment, it is the only image of me that you can accept. It has everything of me within it, because I can never share who I am, in part. I cannot divide what I am. Having received me, I will always be present with you and for you. You are unable to return this message to me, because what I give is forever. You would also be unable to return it to me because we are undivided. You keep what you return. To reject this message would be to deny my existence. This would be a denial of your Self. It is simply impossible. Doing so would violate your existence. You would cease to live. You cannot return your *Life*.

'All life shall persist.'

Because the ultimate nature of existence is oneness and unity, *you* are in truth, the *Home* you seek. *Home* is closer than close. It is *here* and *now*. There is truthfully nothing keeping you from *Home*, but your decision to forget it. In this effort, there is only you. You are the answer you seek. You are your own happiness, your truth. Realizing the truth of this, your freedom is established.

Reality could never take away what has always been yours, unless you allowed for it. It is powerless, without you. *Reality* holds no meaning aside from that with which you have invested in it. Since we remain undivided, what I possess is yours as well. You are stronger than you realize, and when we choose together, the choice is accomplished. Nothing can stand in its way. I do not choose with your person. When you wish, or want for things in *Reality*, the results remain there and the choice holds little or no creative power. I cannot support its choices unless they happen to coincide with my own. That is one reason you feel powerless within *Reality*. Align your choices with mine through your Self, and reclaim what is yours. Your Self will reveal the choices we share. These are our very thoughts.

Return to an awareness of truth.

As One, I am you.
As One, you are me.
As One, we are equally the other, your Self and *The*
***Gathering*.**
Here and now, is *Home*.

Epilogue

We are *The Gathering*. *The One* speaks truthfully. Its creation is beyond our current understanding, but its presence offers us evidence of something more. Because we no longer search or learn, that which exists beyond our knowing must reveal Itself to us. This is the only way we are able to gather additional knowledge. We are aware of the presence of *The One*, but have no immediate knowledge of its creator.

You have all you need. This message is now complete for you. Our presence will continue to guide you, but not in this form. Your perception is now capable of providing you with the information you need. The others, as your Self, will continue to present you with a reflection of your progress, as you complete the journey to *The Reference Point.* Many wait in anticipation of your arrival. *Word's* presence is greatly needed.

As *The Revealing* presents itself, you will quickly recognize your role in assisting others through the transformation. Your own experiences will provide you with answers to many questions. The answers will emerge gradually, as you process these experiences. Processing will happen during and following the event. Time will enable you in this.

Balance activity with rest, interaction with solitude.
Allow for *The Unexpected.*

Glossary

Home - your Self, *The Gathering*, *The One*, unity, freedom, truth

Life - being alive and aware, existence

Program - Your plan for this lifetime, not written 'in stone', God's Will for you, your Dharma

The Revealing - a brief remembrance of everything, everyone, all of it; similar to an apocalypse, but less cataclysmic, *Word* can be present

Word - a force, or entity that exists beyond duality. It arrives when a sufficient number of individuals are in agreement for the purpose of the common good. Its presence facilitates the achievement of the group's purposes.

The One - created out of the event of *The Gathering's* unification; greater than the combination of the elements that went into its creation; *The One* witnesses, knowing only truth

The Reference Point - a place from which to begin, with eyes wide open and seeing beyond the illusion of *Reality* - a point when *The Gathering* is no longer need as guide

The Attention Space - the present moment and immediate concern within your thinking. This space appears to be limited

Reality - the lifetime and place that one appears to be experiencing, Maya (the illusion)

The Gathering - a collection of beings, similar in nature to angels or aliens

The Pretender - the master actor

The Eight - eight of many current archetypes within *Reality*, they guide and assist with the acting, presented in Article Three (Carri, Alyia, Nazahah, Anak, Ayah, Ebed, Aman, and Rapha)

The *original* - something or someone of which there is only one.

The *cause* - the origin of things and events; it is elusive

Strong moments - 'peak experiences,' religious or mystical experiences

Perception: the five, physical senses; enhanced by a connection with your Self

The Invisibles: non-visible beings who have already reached *The Reference Point* and decided to stay and assist with *The Revealing*, before going *Home*.

The Halfway Point: All the important facts about *Reality* and how it works, exist at the *halfway point*. It's very near the area where we both enter *Reality* and return from our experience of a lifetime.

Identicals: naturally-occurring, identical people and objects in *Reality*.

Heartfelt gratitude for recent and enduring encouragement:

Nolan Hurd, Leyna Sanger, Lindsay Parker, Melora Nivienne, Emily York, Elle Koumi, Geronimo's café, Merrickville Book Emporium, B&H Grocery, Singing Pebble Books, Pranashanti Yoga Centre, Marianne Williamson, Brit Elders, Shirley MacLaine, my facebook and Twitter friends, The North Grenville Public Library, McDonalds McCafe coffee, Apple Computers.

About the Author

Michael lives in Ontario, Canada, with his son. He continues to write, while encouraging his students in the discovery of self and other.

His relevant personal and professional background experiences include:
*   15 years as a teacher of Ethics, Philosophy, Religious education and English;
*   Previously published article 'Near Eternal' in the *Journal of the Theosophical Society – Quest;*
*   Previously published article 'Quantum Ascendency' in *Tone Magazine;*
*   Five years living/working in the Kingdom of Saudi Arabia, with excursions to nearby countries that include India, Thailand, and Egypt;
*   Baccalaureate of Arts in Psychology/Religion and Baccalaureate of Education;
•   Meditation instructor and proponent: thespacewithin.podomatic.com

Contact: enterthewitness@gmail.com

www.ingramcontent.com/pod-product-compliance
Lightning Source LLC
LaVergne TN
LVHW091156080426
835509LV00006B/708